RADICALLY REFRAMING CLIMATE CHANGE

RADICALLY REFRAMING CLIMATE CHANGE

A Guide to Saving Ourselves

WILL HACKMAN

BLOOMSBURY ACADEMIC
NEW YORK • LONDON • OXFORD • NEW DELHI • SYDNEY

BLOOMSBURY ACADEMIC

Bloomsbury Publishing Inc, 1359 Broadway, New York, NY 10018, USA
Bloomsbury Publishing Plc, 50 Bedford Square, London, WC1B 3DP, UK
Bloomsbury Publishing Ireland, 29 Earlsfort Terrace, Dublin 2, D02 AY28, Ireland

BLOOMSBURY, BLOOMSBURY ACADEMIC and the Diana logo are trademarks of Bloomsbury Publishing Plc

First published in the United States of America 2026

Copyright © Charles Hackman, 2026

Cover design by Jen Huppert Design
Cover images: @ Getty / Andriy Onufriyenko

All rights reserved. No part of this publication may be: i) reproduced or transmitted in any form, electronic or mechanical, including photocopying, recording or by means of any information storage or retrieval system without prior permission in writing from the publishers; or ii) used or reproduced in any way for the training, development or operation of artificial intelligence (AI) technologies, including generative AI technologies. The rights holders expressly reserve this publication from the text and data mining exception as per Article 4(3) of the Digital Single Market Directive (EU) 2019/790.

Bloomsbury Publishing Inc does not have any control over, or responsibility for, any third-party websites referred to or in this book. All internet addresses given in this book were correct at the time of going to press. The author and publisher regret any inconvenience caused if addresses have changed or sites have ceased to exist, but can accept no responsibility for any such changes.

A catalog record for this book is available from the Library of Congress.

ISBN: HB: 979-8-8818-4266-6
ePDF: 979-8-7651-5568-4
eBook: 979-8-7651-5567-7

Typeset by Deanta Global Publishing Services, Chennai, India
Printed and bound in the United States of America

For product safety related questions contact productsafety@bloomsbury.com.

To find out more about our authors and books visit www.bloomsbury.com and sign up for our newsletters.

To the countless men and women who dedicate their lives to public service and try, through policy and the functions of government, to enrich our society for the betterment of all— and not just the few.
And to those who passionately stand up for what they believe in, sometimes against all odds.

CONTENTS

Author's Note viii
Acknowledgments xii
Introduction xiv

1 What It All Means: A Positive Vision of the Future 1
2 The Politics of Energy 13
3 Three Obstacles to Solving Climate Change 33
4 Mythbusting and Perils of the Blame Game 47

Interlude: From Anger to Agency 65

5 Mitigation, Adaptation, Loss, and Damage 69
6 Reframing How We Think about Climate Change 87
7 Reframing How We Talk about Climate Change 107
8 How to Enact Change at the Personal Level 129
9 How to Enact Change at the Local and Community Level 141
10 How to Enact Change at the Federal Level 157

Conclusion 193
Notes 204
Index 229
About the Author 234

AUTHOR'S NOTE

In the final months of writing this book—during the first few months of President Trump's second term—significant policy and political changes came out in rapid-fire succession. These "flood the zone" changes to our bedrock environmental laws and institutions made it difficult to keep up. That was the point. Like many, I was constantly scrambling to digest new Executive Orders on "Beautiful Clean Coal..." and dozens more, trying to understand their impact on our ability to reduce planet-warming emissions, fight climate change, and the direction in which we thought we were going as a society.

Specific policies mentioned throughout this book—for example, details about fossil fuel production on our public lands—may change by the time you read this. One such change took place in the final days of writing: a blow to the Low Income Home Energy Assistance Program (LIHEAP). This program, run by the federal Health and Human Services agency (HHS), assists with home energy bills and weatherization to nearly seven million low-income households. I mention this decades-old program in Chapter 10 as a positive example of how federal, state, and local governments work together to help communities become safer and more resilient to climate-related impacts like extreme heat or cold. However, in April 2025, during a round of drastic "efficiency" cuts to HHS, the staff who oversaw the LIHEAP program were fired. The program itself wasn't cut—it still had $378 million in funding for the year already received by Congress.

But there was no staff left to get the money out the door to the people who needed it, just as we headed into the hottest months of the year.[1]

Also in April 2025, the Trump Administration announced it was considering shrinking six national monuments in the western United States—potentially opening up millions of acres of protected public lands, owned by you and me, to industrial extraction by corporate interests. It's a core message of this book—and a belief I hold deeply—that efforts to protect our public lands and waters can bring us together. They can remind us of what we still have in common. In a time of deep political division, conservation might be one of the last places where shared values still live. Throughout our nation's history, we've seen many examples of bipartisan support for protecting our natural resources—not just for their beauty, but for what they represent: a shared cultural heritage of some of the most pristine lands and waters in the world and the idea that some things are too important to sell off.

So do Trump's actions—like slashing environmental safeguards or for-profit development of our protected natural places—shatter that legacy? Not entirely. But they do expose how fragile it is, and the need for all of us to get involved to ensure it continues for the benefit of future generations.

This book incorporates and responds to many of President Trump's anti-climate and anti-environmental actions. But not just as a checklist of grievances or a to-do list for the next Democratic majority. Instead of playing into the urge to become overwhelmed or consumed by outrage, I ask: Why did these actions resonate with so many? What do they reveal about our blind spots? And most importantly, how do we build something better—something stronger and more inclusive—that won't collapse with the next election? How can we build a more effective advocacy that reaches across the aisle, engages more people, and shifts acceptance and awareness so similar proposals don't come around again?

We are at an important crossroads. The old ways of talking about climate change—guilt, fear, slogans—aren't working. If we want to build real momentum, we need to meet people where they are, reach them with a new and different language, and invite more people into the movement. That means listening more. It means organizing differently. And it means being willing to rethink how we lead—and who we listen to.

We were at this crossroads well before Trump entered his second term. As such, it's partly a distraction to respond to all of Trump's actions—as unprecedentedly detrimental as each may seem. Constantly reacting keeps us from deeply understanding the changes in tactics we must make. It is more productive to instead focus on the overall approach and framing of this administration as a reflection of a very harmful form of politics that prioritizes deregulation and short-term development over environmental protection, public health, and our society's long-term sustainability within the warming world. That's one vision for our future. We can develop another.

In the months and years after this book comes out, we may see many more changes from this administration—or from future ones. New political landscapes will grow. It is in the nature of our institutions to shift, evolve, and sometimes backslide—although, perhaps more rapidly today than we're used to. But here's the good news: that's okay.

No worthwhile book on winning campaigns, movement building, or reframing an issue to reach a broader audience should be made obsolete by the actions of one person or the passage of a few short years. This book's approach is designed to endure. It doesn't rest solely on breaking news, and it doesn't depend on any one political party. Case studies and expert interviews are provided from both inside and outside environmental and climate campaigns. Examples are given that show how certain moments, ideas, and tactics can change everything. But some truths about our motivations and needs do not change. I share how effectively tapping into these can form the foundation of a successful grassroots movement. Underneath it all, we're still human.

I'm not saying recent attacks on environmental laws and norms don't matter. They do. But the biggest barriers to solving climate change aren't technical or policy-related; they're emotional and ideological. These obstacles have proven durable precisely because we haven't yet done enough to connect climate solutions to people's short-term needs, daily realities, and motivations.

This book argues that we can do better. We can root our advocacy in shared, long-term values that rise above our differences. There *is* a path forward that can cut through the noise and distraction of the day and keep us focused. This book is about building support for the policies we desperately need to solve climate change. The pathways for engagement that its chapters provide will show you how we can do this—today, tomorrow, or anytime in the future as we move toward sustainability. We're not there yet, but we haven't failed either. We still have a narrow window of time to get this right if we can get beyond *our* ideologies and out of our own way.

ACKNOWLEDGMENTS

I would like to thank my agent, Sorche Fairbank, who took a chance on this first-time author. She helped me effectively channel my passion to make a difference and steer my rough and disjointed ideas into something that, because of her, became remarkably coherent and focused. I could not have done it without her. I'd like to thank my publisher, Deni Remsberg, who fully supported my vision from the start and brought me into the Bloomsbury family. Because of Deni and Bloomsbury, my message will get out there and find its audience, and I am forever grateful for that. Thank you to my mother, Dr. Martha Craig, who, as a professor and author herself, instilled in me a spirit for reading and writing at a young age and who provided helpful reviews to many previous drafts of this book as it developed over nearly a decade. Thank you to my grandfather, Gordon Alexander Craig, whose middle name I share and whose distinguished published works and life achievements set the standard for literary and professional excellence in my family and whose shoes perhaps I am filling in a very small way by publishing this book. A very special thank you to my wife, Paula, who never stopped believing in me and put up with my long writing days and nights from the start of our relationship, through family vacations, and up until the night before our wedding where, at our rehearsal dinner, I was finally able to announce my book deal—and who then graciously agreed to delay our honeymoon for six months so I could finish it. And a big thank you to all my friends and family who bounced ideas around with me during intense political and policy conversations and, through their experiences and input, became the backbone of all the recommendations this book makes.

INTRODUCTION

I'm a Millennial and I am pissed. Two wars, two global economic catastrophes, and a pandemic before the age of forty combined with a ballooning cost-of-living crisis and crushing student loan debt can do that to a person. But this is just reality now. Work harder, we're told. The American dream will still be attainable someday. All generations have their struggles.

But there's one thing that compounds these challenges that is certainly unequaled to any other time in human history. That is the ticking time bomb of fossil fuel emissions. With that bomb detonating already, Millennials and Gen Zers will be left to deal with the worst of the climate change fallout well after those responsible have passed away. We will know a world that, even in the best-case scenario, will be unrecognizable compared to the one we have today. This is a truth every young person has grown up with, an unavoidable asterisk attached to our future. The X-Factor weighing over our lives.

We talk about young people having "climate anxiety." I have "climate anger." The anger I feel isn't just toward the unfortunate inevitability of how much the world I love, especially the natural world, will change. It's about the greedy, short-sighted, science-denying/science-avoiding, willful ignorance of those who came before, who selfishly traded my future for living it up in their sunset years.

And the thing that really gets me, more than anything, is when our so-called "leaders" act *surprised* when there is an extreme storm or heat event, flood, or fire. Scientists have been telling us exactly what was going to happen for decades. Elected officials' chief responsibility is the safety of their constituents. They have no right to be surprised about climate change; no right to drop the ball on making sure the places we live are prepared. This is the biggest sham ever perpetrated on the American public, and it is happening over and over each year.

Accepting the science and implementing meaningful climate solutions is a requirement for leadership in the twenty-first century. It's not just about "the environment." It's about protecting and building resilience in the places we live. Nowhere is safe. Climate change has become local—as we've seen from the fires in Los Angeles, floods in the mountain towns of western North Carolina, heat waves in Las Vegas, power outages in Houston, and more. But we still have political leaders, as well as many Americans, who mock and question the validity that human-caused emissions intensify global warming. They call climate change a "hoax."

So yeah, I'm pissed about how things have been going, and I'm not alone. Chances are, you're with me. There are seventy-three million of us in my generation, now the largest in the United States; 142 million adding Gen Z. We are ages fourteen to forty-five, and We Demand Change!

Except, do we?

It might be too easy to fall into the trap of blaming every generation other than our own. All Millennials and many Gen Zers can now vote. We are increasingly holding more positions of political and corporate power, driving consumer spending, choosing products to fulfill our daily lives, and gravitating toward comfort and entertainment—just as those before us did. We have the numbers to change all elections to our advantage, but again, do we?

In 2020, we saw the highest election turnout in more than one hundred years, at nearly 70 percent of all eligible voters. However, turnout for 18–29-year-olds was only 50 percent. This drops even further for midterms, state and local elections, and off-year elections. Case in point—in the historically high-turnout 2018 midterms, just 36 percent of voters aged 18–29 cast ballots. Interestingly, in both 2018 and 2020, youth turnout was heralded by pundits as *high*. This was because in both cases the numbers increased by about eleven points from previous cycles. A low bar.

Then in 2024, with democracy, newly passed historic investments in clean energy, and everything else on the line, turnout among 18–29-year-olds *dropped* to just 42 percent of eligible voters—eight points lower than in 2020. Although it's worth noting that Kamala Harris, representing the candidate who would take climate change seriously, received more votes from young people overall than Donald Trump. Still, Trump received a higher percentage of the youth vote than he did in 2020, especially among young men who increased their support by 14 percent over the four-year period.[1] From Biden's turnout numbers in 2020, Harris also performed twelve points worse with young Latinos and nine points worse with young Asian Americans and Pacific Islanders. Even as Harris won young people overall, and even as the data show 18–29-year-olds as an age cohort were the most Democratic in 2024, there were significant shifts right by younger voters, especially voters of color.[2]

What is going on? Well, it turns out young people care about the economy, the border, and all the same issues as previous generations. According to a 2024 focus group by John Della Volpe, who serves as the director of polling at the Harvard Kennedy School's Institute of Politics, "from the earliest focus groups I conducted this year, there was this innate sense that younger people's personal finances were better and would be better under a Trump administration. Nothing the Democrats seemed to do, over the course of the last year, really changed that perspective."[3]

But what about the millions of young voters who care about climate change, who protest and march in the streets and go on strike from their schools demanding change from their leaders? How could youth turnout actually decrease from 2020 to 2024 when they seem so concerned about the future sustainability of our planet? Where did all the "climate voters" go?

Climate change is rarely near the top of the list of reasons why voters cast their ballots. In other words, people may say they "care" about climate change when asked in a vacuum. But stacked against all the other issues they may see as more immediate on election day, climate change on its own does not become a voting priority. This is very important for thinking about how we address the issue.

According to a Gallup poll before the election, climate change was twenty-first out of twenty-two issues voters listed as "extremely" or "very important" to their vote in 2024.[4] Exit polling after the election confirmed just 7 percent of voters said climate change was the most important issue facing the country. (Although this number did increase from 4 percent in 2020.) It's also clear which party voters associate with climate action, as voters who listed climate change as their most important issue supported Harris over Trump by a ten to one margin.⁵

Still, concern over climate change was not the story of the 2024 election, as the results showed. This is despite analysis that a second Trump presidency could add an extra four billion tons to US emissions by the year 2030.⁶ This has led some, like Roger Pielke Jr. of the conservative-leaning think tank American Enterprise Institute, to claim there is no climate voter.⁷

I also think recent elections indicate a deeper phenomenon that is turning people, especially young people, away from engaging in the very institutions they need for their survival.

A 2021 survey of 10,000 young adults (ages sixteen to twenty-five) in ten countries, conducted by researchers at The University of Bath, NYU Langone Health, Stanford Medicine Center, and other institutions, found, "83 percent said people have failed to care for the planet; 75 percent called the future frightening; 39 percent said they're hesitant to have children." More than half of young adults responded that they believed "humanity is doomed." Respondents in this study also described feelings of abandonment and moral injury related to the government's response to climate change. Correlations were shown that indicated "climate anxiety and distress were significantly related to perceived inadequate government response and associated feelings of betrayal."⁸

So, to recap, Gen Zers and Millennials like me (and maybe you) are angry at our political system and feel abandoned by our government. We feel helpless at the seeming inability of our institutions to solve big problems, so we disengage from the process, which then makes us anxious about our future. Meanwhile, the impacts from global warming are rapidly accelerating all around us, which further increases our despair. But if half to two-thirds of us stay at home during the very elections that determine our future, what change can we expect? We want proportional responses to the threats we face from our power structures, but *we* must do more. And we can, which is what led me to write this book.

We can elect more convincing leaders who understand us and hold those accountable who do not. We can engage more and make a change within our local communities. We can learn how to enact change at the federal and even international levels. We can radically reframe the issue of climate change to overcome polarization and partisanship. Rather than disengaging from the corrupt system, we can mobilize and change it from within. As someone who has spent many years building public awareness on important issues and public policy change, and more importantly, as one of your peers, I will show you how.

As I'm writing this, we're facing one of the most anti-climate administrations in history. I get the frustration—the sense that progress is impossible, not just on climate but on so many things that matter. But everything in this book holds true, no matter who's in office. Future administrations may be just as hostile to climate solutions, and we may even lose ground on commitments we've already made. That's why the strategies, messages, and tactics in these pages were chosen—to withstand the test of time, whether we're in a moment of political alignment or fighting an uphill battle.

This book is split into halves: problems and solutions. In defining the first, I show how a lack of collective positive vision for our future—a failure of imagination both from society and our leaders—harms our ability to even identify the solutions we need. I show how the new climate denialism has shifted and is more effective today than it has ever been. How the complexities of our global energy system need to be understood better by climate advocates so that we know how to change it. How the true obstacles to solving climate change aren't scientific, fact-based, or even technological, but rather political, emotional, and ideological. To reinforce this, I bust popular myths used in the climate movement that distract us from real solutions and hold us back from effectively bringing people together. We must keep the activism energy and focus where it belongs.

Next, in presenting solutions, this book expands upon two easy-to-understand frameworks—"mitigation" and "adaptation." These are long-held categories of understanding climate impacts, science, and needs. But I use these terms in new and more personal ways so that you may understand your role in the changing world more directly and now, not far away into the future. I then present necessary and radical reframings of how we *think* and *talk* about climate change. The decades-old climate rallying cries to "Save the Planet" no longer work in our hyper-partisan world. We must cast out what we all know are ineffective messages and move into a "Climate Activism 2.0."

No amount of beating people over the head with images of polar bears or melting glaciers is going to get them to change their minds if they haven't already. These are things most people will never see in their lifetimes, and using these dated and generic climate images may even be increasing our polarization. Our job shouldn't be to convince non-believers; we no longer have that luxury of time. But we can use language tied to their personal interests to get buy-in and results.

When we pare conversations down to the most personal truths, we can bypass ideology and politics. We're hardwired for survival, and for some conversations, we may need to strip things down to those most basic, fundamental, and personal connections and experiences to find common ground.

When Hurricane Katrina hit the Gulf of Mexico in 2005, I was sitting in my college dorm room watching the disaster unfold and knew I had to do something. I drove thirteen hours with two other close friends from Illinois to volunteer at a disaster relief center in Waveland, Mississippi. Waveland received catastrophic winds combined with storm surge. Nearly the entire town was destroyed. I met people who had lost everything and were coming to us desperate for the most basic needs. One woman told me how she had tried to leave ahead of the storm, but in desperation someone had siphoned her car's gas right out of its tank. She was forced to spend the night in her bathtub, pulling a mattress over herself as the waters rose around her.

Katrina was proven to have been made worse by warming waters—this thing I'd started hearing about was somehow connected to human emissions. But, for the first time in my life, I saw the *personal* face of climate change.

Then, a few years after Katrina, I worked as a commercial crab fisherman in Alaska's Bering Sea—one of the most dangerous jobs in the world. The promise of paying off some of my student loans and setting myself up on solid financial ground as world markets melted down in 2008 drove me up there, as did the prospect of adventure. I had already been a commercial salmon fisherman for two seasons during the summers in Alaska prior to that. But I quickly learned how rough it was out on the open ocean in winter.

Ice, wind, freezing rain stung our faces raw. I had to take handfuls of ibuprofen just so I could bend my fingers. Huge waves crashed over the boat and knocked us off our feet. Being out there was exciting, too. But the fish we chased without sleep for days just weren't there in the same numbers they had been in previous years. Desperate to salvage our season, we switched over to long-lining and pushed ever further and harder until a crash ripped our boat open on the remote island of Adak. The meager profits we'd eked out with our blood, sweat, and tears were gone in one disastrous mistake that totaled our boat and came within a few inches of killing us all. Despite all that, I signed on to one more crab boat to finish the season and at least afford my flight home.

What I experienced in Alaska connected me to a rapidly changing ocean and climate. Climate change is shifting fish migration patterns all over the world and disrupting entire industries and communities. I understand this now in my career much better than I did at the time. But I also understand how people from these and similar industries feel, caught in the middle of these changes. I see myself in many of these blue-collar, working-class jobs and empathize with how climate change will make many of these jobs harder.

Katrina and Alaska are two extreme examples of how I have directly experienced a changing climate. They showed me my personal story in relation to the warming world. Knowing my story has turned me into the advocate that I am today. It changed how I understand the issue and think about solutions. I now see the impacts of climate change everywhere I look.

But everyone has been affected in some way or another by climate change. Facing the problems inherent with its wide-ranging consequences presents the largest set of challenging issues in history. Each year of warming makes these problems worse. And we have never been more divided. This is where *Radically Reframing Climate Change* will provide a path forward for empowerment, engagement, and mobilization.

I want to help you find and understand your story. I want you to help others see theirs. How has climate change impacted your life and the lives of all the people you know and love? How has it changed the places you've been? I want you to see those intimate connections to an issue that may still seem so far away or abstract to so many. This is how we build political support for all the solutions we so desperately need.

Throughout this book, data, case studies, and expert interviews are used to provide evidence and best practices for the tools and tactics with which you will be presented. We know how to do this. Against great opposition, we've built successful public awareness campaigns on civil rights, anti-smoking, seat belts, and plenty of other issues. We can do it again.

This book is really about opportunity. It leads with hope and begins by constructing a positive vision of the future worth fighting for, not fear of what happens if we fail. We must build hope. News articles and so many books trumpet our planet's imminent demise—it's a good sales tactic. But if you believe the world is already "on fire" and the future is doomed, what motivation remains?

Too many of us have been convinced the future is bleak and climate change is too big to solve, and as a result, we become paralyzed. We must counter this narrative with a vision for what success looks like.

What happens if we *solve* climate change, or rather, what happens if humanity can truly live sustainably within the natural world? How might we enter a new golden age of human development and ingenuity, of scientific and technological advances? This book will be true to the climate challenges we face but won't further unhelpful climate doomism. In fact, it seeks to be an antidote.

There is so much energy and passion on our side. One of the most important ways we can feel empowered immediately is to truly recognize the strength of our collective Millennial and Gen Z voting bloc—the largest in US history. I will show you how to harness this power toward making change on any issue, large or small.

You may be like so many educated or aware climate-conscious citizens—surprised or horrified at how quickly noticeable change is upon us and how worrisome it is that we're seemingly already past the point of no return. You may be angry at how many people still don't seem willing to believe (or admit) that climate change is real, immediate, or important. I hear you and am one of you. I have spent many years marching in the streets for climate action. I've run national political campaigns and environmental conservation efforts. I've been to the United Nations climate conferences and learned what keeps climate scientists up at night. I've been horrified, felt hopeless, cheated, exhausted, and more. But through all these experiences, I've also learned more about what works and what doesn't.

In this urgent book, I reframe the "climate crisis" as a "humanity crisis," and give you a more direct, personal, and local connection to the changing world around you. You will learn how climate impacts happening close to home, while terrifying, can also add to our ability to raise public concern and calls for action. Action steps are embedded throughout every solution chapter of this book. You will gain clear how-to guides for engagement in combating climate change in your life, your community, and at all levels of government.

Knowledge is power, especially if we want to hold our national and international leaders to account. Federal representatives who operate on the national and international stages are elected by and beholden to us—their constituents. I will show you how (relatively) easy it is to engage with these representatives, albeit with some important caveats and best practices gleaned from my years of experience doing so. You will hear about some cornerstone federal environmental policies making a difference today and how they might be changed (for better or worse). You will also gain a better understanding of environmental justice and how you can become more engaged to help affected communities.

This book focuses primarily on the United States. Climate change is a global problem, but there are reasons to zero in on American actions—or inactions. The United States is uniquely positioned to lead the world out of this crisis, just as we are uniquely responsible for creating it, as you'll soon see. My background is also primarily in US public policy, political campaigns, and advocacy, so I'm here to offer the best guidance based on where my expertise lies. I firmly believe that without US leadership, the world cannot solve climate change. To get there, we still have a lot of work to do to convince many Americans to take the issue seriously.

I hope you are as energized as I am and ready to make a difference against the biggest threat we've ever faced. Ready to turn the tide on polarization, paralysis, anxiety, fear, apathy, doomism, anger, and betrayal. Let's get started.

1

What It All Means
A Positive Vision of the Future

Imagine with me for a moment, a changed but livable world.

You wake up to soft ambient light that gradually increases around your apartment. Window shades, airflow settings, home appliances, and even your coffee pot automatically come out of nightly hibernation and work their magic, conserving energy where they can, as you walk room to room. Filtered, collected water from overnight rain mixes with municipal sources in your pipes as you shower. Climbing into your autonomous electric vehicle (AV), you say "Navigate to Office" and finish breakfast while watching the morning news projected across the interior glass. A relaxing and personalized high-speed ride from your home. No traffic, no accidents, as self-driving vehicles of all shapes and sizes enter and exit roads flawlessly. And the roads—no longer concrete stretches of heat-absorbing black but instead circuitry-filled systems paved with embedded solar panels and mapping sensors that charge and guide AVs along their white heat-reflective surfaces.

It's a hot day, nearly 130°. But as you near the city, a miles-long line of thousands of small wind turbines positioned in the median spins with passing vehicle air displacement, which generates a small breeze in addition to electricity. The AV drops you off at your building entrance and heads to a holding location underground and off the pedestrian-dominated streets. Clinging green vines cover the exterior of the building and connect to balcony gardens filled with additional shrubs, bushes, and flowering trees. The thick green creates a vertical carpet one hundred stories tall and makes the building seem almost organic, alive. It also serves a very important purpose: filtering the air, providing shade, and catching precious rainwater which, these days, usually comes in violent flash floods in between droughts. It's amazing how much used to wash away too quickly, down into the drains and rivers, causing them to overflow. Now what is caught and brought into storage tanks by these plants and other intricate runoff systems keeps the city going during the dry days.

The year is 2100 and global average temperature has increased by 2°C (3.6°F) from the start of the Industrial Revolution a few hundred years prior. The summers are hot, the winters are ice-free in most of the world, sea-level rise has flooded many low-lying countries and coastal cities. Hundreds of millions have had to move. It is a different world from the one we knew at the beginning of the last century. But humanity and nature are thriving. Human-caused greenhouse gases have been reduced to near-net zero after massive decarbonization efforts and with the remaining emissions offset not by carbon credits but vast new areas of thriving forests and carbon-hungry grasses.

This has cleaned the air, saving hundreds of millions of lives from cancer and other cardiovascular or respiratory ailments related to air pollution. Electricity is renewable. All transportation has been electrified. Climate-smart agriculture captures and sequesters more carbon than it emits now. Crops are grown sustainably, regeneratively, and, in some places, vertically. Water is caught, conserved, recycled, and transported around the country where needed in pipeline routes once used for fossil fuels.

Society still exists with many luxuries but in better harmony with the natural world, able to adapt to anything the extremes of a forever-warmed climate can throw. We have pulled back from the brink of climate system collapse. Carbon dioxide is slowly falling out of the atmosphere over time, pulled down by gravity, a trillion newly planted trees, and removal technologies. Humanity has adopted a longer-term, generational planning mentality. We are secure knowing our story will continue for hundreds or even thousands of years longer.

* * *

This story provides a vision of our sustainable future that is nearly the best we can hope for. It's based on realistic and pragmatic technologies already being worked on—some with the power to bring vast and positive change to our lives. But what we need to achieve them is time. If we don't address our current level of warming, we will reach higher temperatures much more quickly. That could lead to mass conflict and disaster well before the end of the century. It's not hyperbole to say that our choices over the next five to ten years could determine our future for generations to come.

Even in my positive scenario, the realities of climate change still exist and have gotten worse. The hardships of sea-level rise, extreme heat, floods, fires, droughts, and more have displaced many tens of millions. But society has taken the steps we needed to survive. Due to collective decarbonization efforts, global average temperature has only risen by the maximum amount allowable within international climate goals. Clean energy and other sustainable practices have been implemented across the economy. Cities and towns have adapted to climate hazards. Continued scientific and technological advancements have given us more comfort and ease with daily routines. Nature-based civil and urban engineering projects have brought greenspaces to even the most congested areas, and cities have been transformed into walkable and bikeable havens.

While still far from perfect, how different is this positive vision of the future from the one so many of us are bombarded with each day?

Television and film endlessly portray a post-apocalyptic future where cities are void of human life and sand dunes stretch to the horizon. Usually, we are to blame for our own demise—bringing about some terrible war, pandemic, ecological disaster, or technology-driven extermination. Sometimes, it's aliens or zombies. These stories generate some of the biggest blockbuster hits every year; we literally can't get enough. Even climate activists engage in this game, with Leonardo DiCaprio's *Don't Look Up* as one example. Many of these stories are merely intended as wake-up calls for what we hope to avoid. We all still believe a better future is possible, right? But combine the abundance of exposure to all these pop culture images on our screens with how public polling says we feel about the future, and it seems like—maybe we *don't*.

A 2024 Georgetown Institute of Politics and Public Service poll found that 81 percent of voters believe democracy in America is being threatened.[1] A 2023 Pew Research Center poll found around six-in-ten US adults believe "life for people like them is worse today than it was 50 years ago," and, looking forward to 2050, a third of US adults "express very little confidence in the country's future."[2] A 2024 poll by the American Psychiatric Association found that more than half of US adults believe climate change is negatively impacting their mental health.[3] This follows a 2020 American Psychiatric Association poll that found two-thirds of Americans (largely correlating to political affiliation) are somewhat or extremely anxious about the impact of climate change on the planet.[4]

Clearly, many of us feel very negative about the future. As Dr. Ayana Elizabeth Johnson writes in her book, *What If We Get It Right?: Visions of Climate Futures*, "goodness do we need more imagination right now, to create clearer visions of desirable climate futures . . . a future we can see ourselves in, where there's a place for us and the communities we hold dear . . . when it comes to better outcomes, we've largely been left hanging. That is a problem."[5]

I agree, and one of my core messages is that we are still in control of the future we wish to create. The technology described is not farfetched, and many of the plans are already in motion.

In places like the United States, the world's highest emitter of climate warming greenhouse gases for 150 years and still the second highest emitter today, coal, one of the highest sources of greenhouse gases, has been in decline—decreasing 30 percent since 1990.[6] Another quarter of the remaining US coal plants are set to retire by the end of this decade.[7] In 2022, the Inflation Reduction Act (IRA) was signed into law and provided $370 billion in new funding to facilitate clean energy projects—the largest such bill in US history. It is estimated that this public-sector funding could leverage upwards of an additional $1–$2 trillion in private-sector funding.

Due to the IRA and other efforts, renewable capacity growth is forecast to double in the United States by 2030.[8] Although these estimates were made before Republicans in Congress passed President Trump's "Big, Beautiful Bill" in July of 2025. As I write this, analysis is still being completed on the far-ranging impacts of this massive bill. But some have already concluded it will effectively crush the IRA and have a devastating effect on US clean energy development. This bill, along with other actions taken by the Trump administration, could also stimulate coal production—more on this in the next chapter.[9]

Still, as I write this in 2025, the politically conservative state of Texas has more installed wind and solar power generation capacity than any other state, Democrat or Republican, by a long shot. Nearly 2.5 times more than California, the next leading state.[10]

Globally, the International Energy Agency (IEA) forecasts that between 2024 and 2030, the world is set to add more than 5,500 gigawatts (GW) of new renewable energy capacity—almost three times the increase seen over the previous six-year period. To put 5,500 GW into context, it is roughly equal to the total power capacity of China, the European Union, India, and the United States combined in the year 2023. According to the IEA's Executive Director Fatih Birol,

> renewables are moving faster than national governments can set targets for. This is mainly driven not just by efforts to lower emissions or boost energy security—it's increasingly because

renewables today offer the cheapest option to add new power plants in almost all countries around the world. . . . By 2030, we expect renewables to be meeting half of global electricity demand.[11]

These numbers provide many points of optimism and stand in undeniable contrast to the feeling so many of us have that nothing is being done or that all our recent gains are now being rolled back. It is true that fossil fuels are still among us and will be for some time. But the clean energy revolution has already begun in the United States and the world, even in places where the politics of climate change may not be widely accepted. From a business standpoint, clean energy just makes sense. In many places, wind and solar have become cheaper than coal, which is the dirtiest and highest climate-polluting form of electricity generation. The cost per unit of energy generated by renewable sources has fallen dramatically over the last forty years, especially for wind and solar. Technological breakthroughs and forward-thinking public policies have paved the way.[12]

We can feel even better if we know where all this investment is taking us. The 2015 international Paris climate Agreement provides a helpful blueprint. Implemented by 196 countries, this is the framework that seeks to bring all countries together to collectively solve the problem of global warming. I will come back to the Paris Agreement throughout this book to ground us in how we should be thinking about the goals we're working toward. Clean energy standards, power plant regulation, fuel efficiency standards for cars and trucks, and renewable energy investments in wind or solar are all part of achieving climate stability. These are some of the many domestic actions that contribute to broader Paris Agreement goals.

But we determine the policies we put in place in our country, not the other way around—despite what some naysayers of international agreements like to say.

The US plan—the sum total of all our domestic efforts to reduce greenhouse gas emissions—is known as our "Nationally Determined Contribution," in global climate speak. Since each NDC covers roughly five-year time spans, you can find the first two that the United States submitted online, which reflect our decarbonization goals from now through 2030. Every other country's plan can also be found online. Future submissions will take the most up-to-date science into consideration, evaluate our progress, and ratchet up ambition as needed. This is how we get a sense of where we are today and where we still need to be.

Now, I know what you're thinking. "Didn't President Trump pull us out of the Paris Agreement in 2025?" "How can we still make progress under global climate goals we're not even part of?"

Well, we've seen this movie before.

A few months into his first term in 2017, Trump announced his intent to withdraw from the Paris Agreement. Just two years prior, the United States had taken a leadership role in getting the agreement over the finish line. Now, a change in administration was signaling a potential new era of American climate isolationism.

Four days later, on June 5, and in response to Trump's actions which had been anticipated by many, a broad coalition formed of governors, mayors, universities, faith leaders, and corporations that represented more than half the entire US economy and population.[13] They called themselves the "We Are Still In" coalition, and they committed their states, towns, and businesses to staying in the Paris Agreement, regardless of the actions of the federal government.

The coalition attended the official United Nations climate negotiations "on behalf of" the United States, setting up their own "United States Climate Action Center." I attended the 2017 United Nations Climate Change Conference in Bonn, Germany—known colloquially as "COP23." There, I heard Republican Jim Brainard, Mayor of Carmel, Indiana, sum up We Are Still In's mission as he addressed a packed crowd,

> What I can tell you is that the United States is going to meet our Paris Agreement goals—with or without the federal government—cities and states are going to get it done. It's important to point out to people from other countries that mayors and governors have a lot of power in the United States. Just because the federal government isn't acting, we can still act.[14]

I attended COP23 on behalf of the Washington, DC-based Georgetown Climate Center, which led a bipartisan delegation from eleven US states. Our delegation included four governors, state legislators, and heads of state environmental and energy agencies. Between We Are Still In and the Georgetown Climate Center, 2017 saw the then-largest attendance of US state and local representatives at any UN climate talks over the previous twenty-two years. Nonstop events were held to highlight climate policies being passed at the city, state, and corporate levels to incentivize clean energy production and reduce emissions. This was a direct response to Trump's negative actions, and unfortunate that it was needed. However, the shift in focus and recalibration of climate policies to cities and states was a positive development in the long run. It was also truly inspiring to see a completely different reality from what the common wisdom was back home—as headline after headline focused on Trump's environmental and climate rollbacks.

Does this example paint a different picture of what was happening at the time from what you may have thought? It is true that a failure of federal leadership for four years set us back then as it is again now. But where were the positive stories of these local leaders coming together to keep America on track?

History is repeating itself as President Trump once again ordered the United States to withdraw from the Paris Agreement on the first full day of his second term. Once again, a change in administration is hindering our ability to address the immediacy of climate impacts and develop solutions. A lack of federal leadership is a huge blow at a critical time when scientists are telling us we must be rapidly decarbonizing by 2030 to avoid the worst catastrophic impacts from warming. The next administration won't even be sworn in until right before this deadline—and that's assuming they are friendly to immediate climate action (and have the votes in Congress to get it done).

But cities, states, corporations, universities, and more kept their commitments strong under Trump's first term. These subnational actors have the ability to pass their own state and local policies or corporate policies that affect their supply chains. We are seeing this play out again under Trump's second term. Future chapters expand on subnational action in much more detail. But we have seen a sustained shift to cities and states staying strongly committed to climate action despite federal action. This is particularly true in Democratic areas, but there are many Republican examples as well.

* * *

Lessons learned from these short examples show there is much we can do to keep moving forward—no matter what friendly or unfriendly, government we fall under at any given point in time. The Paris Agreement and the yearly United Nations climate negotiations will continue. Many cities and states will keep going and making commitments, with or without federal involvement.

But all of this takes constant pressure. Change doesn't happen on its own. If we lose one campaign, we build the next. If certain tactics don't work, we come up with more effective ones. It is our responsibility, as climate advocates and activists, to create new ideas that connect with more people and increase public support. No one is helped by us futilely screaming into the wind. We mustn't cave to the apocalyptic visions of the future we love to hate-watch when things don't go our way. #Resist works to defend the progress we've already made. It's an important fallback in tough times. But what work are we doing to build the *smarter* campaign with the forward-looking vision we need to get us out of this partisan back-and-forth war?

To do this work, we must remain optimistic. I am an optimist, even through negative political setbacks. Pessimism is the easy way out, an escape, a way to throw up your hands and let yourself off the hook from doing the hard work, to move the goalposts and never be wrong if things don't go your way. As Dr. Hannah Ritchie explains in her book, *It's Not the End of the World: How We Can Be the First Generation to Build a Sustainable Planet,*

The problem is that people mistake optimism for "blind optimism," the unfounded faith that things will just get better. Blind optimism is dumb. And dangerous. If we sit back and do nothing, things will not turn out fine... Optimism is seeing challenges as opportunities to make progress; it's having the confidence that there are things we can do to make a difference. We can shape the future, and we can build a great one if we want to.[15]

We face real obstacles standing in the way of climate solutions; in the way of the vision of sustainability this chapter began with. These obstacles come from both outside and inside the climate movement. I define them in Chapter 3 in new ways that, even if you're familiar with this topic, might not be what you think. Understanding and overcoming each of them will be critical to building our winning campaign on the issue of climate change.

But before we get there, we must first confront global energy and the new climate denialism that centers around it. This book is about radical reframings and radical change. And there is no question that radical change *is* needed in our global energy supply. As David Spratt wrote in his report *Collision Course: 3 Degrees of Warming and Humanity's Future,*

> In any crisis, facing the world as it really exists is the first step on the road to actions that have the capacity to solve the problem. Public health education campaigns—such as on smoking, AIDS, skin cancer and COVID—have all demonstrated the efficacy of being brutally honest about the problem in order to engage people about the often inconvenient solutions. Climate is no different.[16]

2

The Politics of Energy

The New Denialism

There is a new and growing form of climate denialism that hinges upon the so-called "reality" of our current energy system being too big and too difficult to change so quickly, especially as global demand grows and especially if we wish to keep costs low. "Environmentalists don't understand energy markets; their policies will lead to blackouts and take us 'backward'; the *cost* of solving climate change is just too great and will put too much burden on hard-working average citizens," or so the arguments go.

This is very different from the early days of deniers trying to dismiss scientists or calling climate change a hoax. Next, they offered a begrudging "yes, the climate is changing, but we don't know to what extent *humans* are responsible for it." And now we've progressed to "okay, climate change is happening, and it's probably being made worse by humans. But it's just too expensive to fix and you don't want your bills to go up do you?"

By reframing the issue around cost and fear of what *you* may have to give up, the new denialism has gotten more dangerous. Even slight increases in cost can be a huge negative motivator for people, especially during election time. Even for those voters who list climate as an important issue, research shows they are generally unwilling to pay extra for it.[1] But this framing also appeals to people's fear of change, fear of the unknown, and a sense of how much easier it would be just to stick with the status quo—with what we know; the path of least resistance. The new denialism does everything it can to present a vision of the fossil-free future as one of energy insecurity, rolling blackouts, backward progress on the comforts and standards of living we've gotten used to in the Western industrialized world, and unaffordability.

The reality is, renewables like solar and wind are already cost-competitive with fossil fuels in many places. For instance, in 2023, the global weighted average cost of producing one unit of electricity over the lifetime of new onshore wind projects—known as its Levelized Cost of Energy or LCOE—was 67 percent lower than the weighted average LCOE of fossil fuel projects. The global weighted average LCOE of solar PV was 56 percent less than fossil fuel projects.[2] This is a stunning decline in price for wind and solar over the last fifteen years—led by improvements in manufacturing and supply chain infrastructure as well as huge leaps in the efficiency of new projects. And cost isn't just about dollars. It also affects your health, food supply, and safety—three things that will be severely and negatively impacted by a world in which fossil fuel emissions continue to be emitted at the levels they are today. But none of that matters if we can't get people to listen. We must study the popular attacks from the fossil fuel industry and learn how to counter their false narratives more effectively. We can't allow the fossil fuel industries and interests to claim they are the only ones who understand the complexities of energy and therefore are the only ones to dictate policy decisions.

This means that you, the grassroots activist, need to learn. This stuff is complicated, so bear with me. I want to equip you with some critical information and messages that will not only help you gain a clear-eyed understanding of our current system but also make you a better advocate for realistic climate solutions.

Growing Global Energy Demand

The International Energy Agency (IEA) projects that by 2030, renewables will supply half of the world's electricity. That is an astonishing scale-up from where we were just ten years ago. But that also means fossil fuels will still be meeting the other half. And if you zoom out to total energy needs—including electricity generation, transportation, heavy industry, and everything else—some estimates say fossil fuels will still be supplying half of it globally, even through 2050.[3] Why? Because energy demand keeps growing as the world's population grows and developing nations industrialize. And that's not necessarily bad—economic growth improves people's lives. But it also means more cars, more trucks, more heating and cooling, more everything.

As a result, the US Energy Information Administration (EIA) forecasts rising demand for oil and natural gas through 2050, even alongside the rapid expansion of renewables and electric vehicles. And many of these estimates don't yet factor in the surging energy needs of data centers and mining operations fueling the AI and cryptocurrency revolutions.

Roughly one hundred million barrels of oil are produced around the world each day now. The EIA projects that by 2050, 120 million barrels will be produced per day. They also project, at least for now and absent major new policy decisions, that energy-related CO_2 emissions will continue to increase through 2050.[4]

The Energy Addition

These numbers are a snapshot in time and can change. We will explore options in future chapters that could greatly influence outcomes over the next few decades. But as these energy agencies and other independent studies show, the increasingly larger scale deployments of renewables are currently *not* replacing fossil fuels. They are instead expanding the overall amount of energy available to meet the needs of growing demand. This has caused some to consider the term "energy *transition*" misleading and more accurate to refer to what's going on as an "energy *addition*."[5] In fact, previous energy transitions over the past 200 years—from wood to oil to coal to gas—were similar energy additions as overall energy demand only continued to increase through each of these periods.

These points are well-known to the US industry association for oil and gas, the American Petroleum Institute (API). They look at growing global demand as proof that fossil fuels will be needed far into the future and argue that supply should come from the United

States. They cite the same energy agency reports as validation of, as they describe it, "the reliable, affordable energy provided by natural gas and oil."[6]

It is hard to argue with demand projections as they currently stand. As the environmental organization Friends of the Earth states on their campaign website to phase out fossil fuels, "without a planned, equity-oriented transition away from fossil fuels, no amount of clean energy permitting will stave off the accelerating climate crisis."[7] In other words, transitioning away from fossil fuels requires *more* than just the growth of renewables.

"Drill Baby Drill"

Slogans like "drill baby drill" continue to come from some politicians even as the impacts of climate change rise around us. How can they *be* so tone-deaf? Certainly, there is a huge amount of entrenched economic interest and lobbying influence in keeping things status quo. Those forces should never be underestimated. But there is also a convincing pro-fossil fuel story for those looking at demand.

Fossil fuel companies, and the politicians who support them the most, may even try to argue a moral high ground as increased energy access indeed leads to better standards of living—which hundreds of millions around the world still urgently need. Of the seventeen United Nations Sustainable Development Goals, number seven, Energy, is a requirement for almost every other one. You cannot have healthcare, education, food, sanitation, infrastructure, or anything else that we consider the pillars of modern developed societies without affordable energy.

However, reject the claims that development and affordable energy can *only* occur through increased fossil fuel use. There is a cognitive term called "recency bias" that explains how we may give too much importance to recent events when thinking about future trajectories that may not play out the same way. On the one hand, you could use this to say we shouldn't rush to be too optimistic about recent climate progress—for instance, the decline of coal use in the United States or the rapid expansion of renewables—as it may not take future demand for fossil fuels, or the impact of rollbacks from an aggressively anti-climate president, into consideration.

But you can also use recency bias to challenge the narrative of the fossil fuel industries. Development can, and already does, occur with renewable energy. The recent golden age for oil and gas observed over the last few decades does not dictate our future. Most people don't care where their energy comes from as long as it comes, is affordable, and reliable. And renewables now offer the cheapest option for adding new electricity generation capacity in almost all countries around the world.[8]

We can achieve a first-of-its-kind energy transition, where renewables not only supplement but replace the vast majority of fossil fuels. But this will require economic pressure and strong governmental regulatory actions that—and this is crucial—actively *suppress* fossil fuel usage. For the limited cases where fossil fuels and petroleum products will still be necessary in the long term, we must develop new technologies that can effectively capture and store their emissions.

The Problem of US Supply

Our honest conversation about growing global energy demand must also examine our choices right here at home. From 2009 to 2015, US crude oil production roughly doubled, due in large part to the boom in shale oil production and advancements in drilling technologies (such as hydraulic fracturing or "fracking"). In 2018, the United States became the largest producer of oil in the world. In 2023, the United States produced 21.91 million barrels of oil per day—accounting for 22 percent of global output and exceeding the production of Saudi Arabia, the second highest producer, by ten million barrels per day.[9] The United States has nearly one million oil and gas wells and over 2.6 million miles of pipelines—enough to wrap around the Earth 104 times or travel to the Moon eleven times.[10] For the past six consecutive years, the United States has produced more crude oil than any nation at any time in history.[11]

And it doesn't stop there.

The United States is also the number one producer of natural gas in the world, by far, accounting for nearly 25 percent of total global production.[12]

The fossil fuel industry is incredibly entrenched. Trillions of dollars of investment carry the expectation that new plants and pipelines will operate and pay dividends for decades into the future. Such a system won't be shut down without a compelling reason, which will likely require government regulation. But the United States government today is, by any metric, not only perpetuating the global fossil fuel system, it's also dominating it. And yet, many Americans have been led to believe the opposite—that we're somehow "losing" the energy race and drastic action needs to be taken before we can no longer turn our lights on or drive ourselves to work.

Recent actions our government has taken may ensure we lose the *clean* energy race, and specifically lose it to China—which is more than happy to sell solar panels, wind turbines, EVs, batteries, and green technologies to the world as we push fossil fuels. But we are not in danger of running out of energy writ large any time soon.[13]

The "Energy Emergency"

The term "Energy Independence" has long been a political catchphrase in Washington, DC, championed by pro-fossil fuel politicians who argue that the United States should produce enough energy to meet its own needs—an idea that seems straightforward. However, many conservatives contend that Democratic administrations' climate-focused clean energy policies undermine energy independence, making the United States more reliant on foreign energy. They view their support for domestic fossil fuel production as both realistic and pragmatic. To signal this stance, they frequently use the phrase "all of the above" to advocate for increased fossil fuel use, framing it as a counterpoint to Democratic and activist calls for reducing fossil fuels and expanding clean energy sources.

Following this playbook, on the first day of his second term, President Trump signed multiple executive orders concerning energy. In these, he declared an "energy emergency," claiming the Biden administration's policies had harmed domestic energy production, led to inadequate supply, and devastated American consumers by driving up costs. Trump vowed to "unleash American energy," defining it narrowly as being limited to oil, gas, coal, nuclear, and certain alternative sources like geothermal and biofuels. Notably, renewable sources like solar and wind were excluded in his definition of American energy—despite the fact that US solar and wind industries employed over 430,000 workers in all fifty states in 2024, and wind alone employs nearly twice as many people as the coal industry.[14]

A parallel Presidential Memo (similar to an Executive Order for all practical purposes) also paused new offshore wind leasing in federal waters and ordered a review of existing leases and permitting practices.[15] The review of recently permitted projects already underway (and their potential termination) was particularly concerning to wind companies that had significant sunk capital costs. This uncertainty comes on top of rising interest rates, tariff threats, and supply chain issues, all of which are casting doubt on the future of the US offshore wind industry.

This would also be a huge blow from a climate perspective. According to Oceana, offshore wind could supply 50 to 100 percent of all the electricity needed for seven states and over 20 percent of at least three more. Collectively, just this one form of renewable energy could supply nearly half of all the power needed for the entire East Coast.[16] Further, Oceana states, "Developing 127 gigawatts offshore wind energy capacity over 20 years would provide energy at a cost of about $36 billion less than the production of economically recoverable new offshore oil and natural gas on the Atlantic coast," and "could create between 133,000 and 212,000 jobs annually in the United States—more than three times more jobs than new offshore oil and natural gas development is expected to create."[17] Of course, Trump's pause and review of offshore wind did not apply to offshore oil, gas, or minerals extraction.[18]

At the time of Trump's orders, there was little evidence that the United States was facing an imminent energy emergency. In addition to the United States already being the largest producer of oil and natural gas in the world, the price of oil was at roughly the same average cost it had been for decades (adjusted for inflation) and the cost of a gallon of gasoline was close to a three-year low.[19] Given these facts, there was also little evidence that oil companies would immediately start drilling a bunch more as a direct result of Trump's actions. These companies benefit from a higher price-per-barrel and don't want to oversaturate the market, potentially decreasing the price. Although I'm sure they appreciated the gesture.

That said, electricity demand is increasing here at home just as it is around the world. According to some estimates, the US population will increase by more than twenty million people in 2030 over 2020 census levels. Our electricity grid is aging, leading to wasted power and making it more prone to failures. This is compounded by increased heat waves alongside other climate-driven disasters, like hurricanes, which can overwhelm the grid. And a new report from the EIA projects US power consumption in 2025 and 2026 will reach record levels, driven in part by rising demand from data centers.[20] So there is some reason for concern if nothing is done.[21]

But we were doing something. Because of the Inflation Reduction Act and other clean energy incentives passed in recent years, hundreds of gigawatts of new clean energy capacity were projected to be added to the US grid over the next ten to twenty years. Trump's

"Big Beautiful Bill" cut many of these incentives, which could kill these projects.[22] Then there's the pausing of offshore wind leases and the intentional uncertainty being sown across that entire industry by this administration. Why would you do this if you believe we're in an energy emergency? These disastrous actions could actually threaten our ability to meet our growing electricity needs and increase costs for us as consumers.

As for rapidly deploying new fossil fuel capacity, here's a question worth considering: "What level of oil and gas production is necessary for energy independence if we are already producing exponentially more than any other country?"

There is no answer. There is no amount that would be "enough." There is only the narrative of those who wish to endlessly increase fossil fuels for the sake of profits, even at the expense of our sustainable future. Meanwhile, political opponents score points by labeling everything the other side does as "bad" and presenting their own solutions as the only "good" ideas, even if that means manufacturing a crisis where none exists or taking actions that actually *do* create a crisis—simply because you had a bone to pick with the actions of your predecessor.

Regarding claims that Democratic administrations make us more energy dependent, consider that Democrat Barack Obama oversaw the fracking boom that doubled US oil production. He also signed into law the repeal of the oil export ban in 2015 that has now made the United States a dominant fossil fuel exporter. Obama took these steps to support fossil fuels at nearly the exact same time his administration was getting the Paris international climate Agreement over the finish line and even as his administration championed strong climate policies at home like the Clean Power Plan and strict emissions standards for cars and trucks. Obama believed in the science of global warming and took decarbonization seriously; he wrote the plan for the United States to decarbonize by mid-century, in line with Paris Agreement goals.[23] In hindsight, President Obama's contradictory support for both fossil fuels and clean energy are hard to reconcile for many climate activists. But it showed one thing—clearly there is space for climate and clean energy progress even under an all-of-the-above administration, which the Obama administration actually was in practice.

The Biden administration exceeded Obama in passing even more historic climate and clean energy policies. In 2023, new clean energy jobs accounted for more than half of all new jobs in the US energy sector, growing at twice the rate of the overall US economy—a direct result of Biden's Inflation Reduction Act and Bipartisan Infrastructure Law.[24] There is no doubt that Biden was the most climate-friendly US president in history.

Did this hurt our energy independence and lead to an emergency? Not likely. In 2023, the United States produced 22 million barrels of oil per day while consuming only 20 million barrels per day—suggesting theoretical independence. But then we exported 10 million barrels per day and imported 8.5 million barrels per day.[25] Oil is a global commodity, and whatever makes the most profit will be done. But the point remains, policies that promote clean energy do not hurt our ability to produce fossil fuels. Although, to solve global climate change, perhaps they need to.

* * *

Before we move on . . . a short note on coal . . . An April 2025 Executive Order titled "Reinvigorating America's Beautiful Clean Coal Industry," designated coal as a "national priority." It also made coal "essential to our national and economic security," vowed to roll back any regulations that "undermine coal production," and sought to dramatically increase domestic production and exports. The order designated coal as a mineral—which it is not—so that other orders related to increasing US mineral production would also benefit coal. One of the stated purposes of the order was to use coal as a critical energy source to meet the rising US electricity demand from AI data processing centers.[26]

Let's get real. Coal is the dirtiest and deadliest source of energy, killing hundreds of thousands of people around the world every year.[27] A 2023 study from researchers at the Harvard School of Public Health, George Mason University, and University of Texas at Austin found that, from 1999 to 2020, nearly half a million deaths in the United States were attributable to coal particulate matter 2.5—a deadly air pollutant that penetrates deep into the lungs. At its peak, deaths from PM2.5 air pollution attributable to the 480 coal-fired power plants operating in the United States during the time period of the study averaged more than 43,000 per year. Just ten of those coal plants contributed to a staggering 5,000 deaths each. In the final years of the study's time period, deaths had declined to around 1,600 per year—roughly where it is today—due in part to coal plants installing scrubbers but also largely because many plants shut down.[28] Today, there are roughly 200 coal plants left in the United States, with half of these set to retire over the next five to ten years.[29]

Even at reduced numbers, coal-fired power plants continue to be the largest source of mercury pollution in the United States and the largest industrial source of toxic water discharges into our rivers and streams. Wastewater from coal plants dumps mercury, arsenic, lead, and other toxins into the drinking water for tens of millions of Americans.[30] This led the EPA in 2024 to create a new rule that would put stricter standards on water pollution from coal plants and prevent over 600 million pounds of these toxins from being dumped each year into US waterways.[31] In 2025, however, President Trump's EPA announced it would reconsider these guidelines to "help unleash American energy."[32]

Even more than environmental regulation, however, innovation and market factors that made natural gas more cost-effective have contributed to coal's decline in the United States. Natural gas now supplies more than 2.5 times more US electricity generation than coal and, while still a fossil fuel we need to transition away from, burns much cleaner.[33] Switching to natural gas over coal has led to at least some progress in reducing US emissions over the past twenty years. Even so, coal is *still* the largest single source of greenhouse gas emissions in the US electricity sector. Globally, coal contributes nearly half of all planet-warming carbon dioxide emissions from the burning of fossil fuels each year.[34] In the short term, reinvesting in coal gives us no foot to stand on in conversations we wish to have with other countries to reduce their emissions as they industrialize. In the long term, it threatens our health and the future stability of our climate.

The United States has the largest proven and recoverable coal reserves of any country—nearly one quarter of the entire world's reserves.[35] Our reserves are 348 times our consumption. So if we wanted to increase production, we absolutely could.[36] But there is no such thing as "beautiful and clean coal." Even with the improved safety standards we've implemented in our plants, if we increase production for the sake of exports, then other countries might be burning our coal in their plants with fewer standards. We will simply be contributing to more deaths in those countries.

"Foreign Oil," Energy Security, and Exporting Climate Change

Another important part of our conversation about growing energy needs and policies that seek to meaningfully transition us away from fossil fuels is the term "energy security." This is where we typically think of things like "foreign oil" and our historical dependence on countries that don't share our democratic values. And while I am old enough to remember entire wars that were started in the Middle East mostly over oil, times have changed.

In 2023, 63 percent of the petroleum we imported came from our North American neighbors and allies, Canada and Mexico, while just 16 percent came from the Organization of the Petroleum Exporting Countries (OPEC)—Iraq, Saudi Arabia, Venezuela, and others. That's more than 30 percent drop in our reliance on OPEC since 2001—a positive shift since their ability to manipulate supply can disrupt global markets and hurt the US economy.[37] ("Petroleum" includes crude oil and refined products like gasoline, jet fuel, diesel, kerosene, biofuels, and other essential fuels and feedstocks.)

So, okay, this is where I can understand energy independence advocates saying higher production at home leads to decreased reliance on other countries' oil and increased energy security for us. But as our domestic production has grown astronomically to meet the needs of our consumption, so too have our exports.

Between 1975 and 2015, the United States maintained a ban on crude oil exports until Congress repealed it. Ten years later, we have become one of the largest exporters of both crude oil and refined petroleum products—shipping 10.15 million barrels per day to 173 countries. Mexico and China were the top destinations of US petroleum exports—receiving 21 percent. In 2023, we even exported 30,000 barrels per day of petroleum *to* OPEC countries.[38]

Natural gas exports also increased year over year for the ninth consecutive year in 2023. The United States is now the largest exporter of Liquefied Natural Gas (LNG) in the world.[39] Finally, although US coal production and consumption have declined since its peak in 2008, the United States exported 86 million short tons of coal in 2022 (about 14 percent of our total production) to 71 countries, with India receiving 20 percent of these exports.[40] And, if recent pro-coal actions in the United States have any success, coal exports (and associated emissions) could increase even further, even if our own domestic consumption does not.

Taken together, greenhouse gas emissions from total US fossil fuel exports—from production to global shipping to burning—have increased nearly 500 percent since 2005. By 2030, this could grow even further and contribute a whopping 2.9 gigatons of planet-warming greenhouse gases annually—the equivalent of the entire country of India's emissions in the year 2019.[41] Efficiency standards, clean energy policies, and the decline of domestic coal consumption are slowly reducing greenhouse gases within US borders. But we are now contributing to the greenhouse gases of nearly every other country on Earth. The cost from climate damages attributable to US fossil fuel exports alone could reach trillions of dollars over the next few decades.[42]

It might make sense to see narrow carve outs for continued long-term US fossil fuel imports and exports for global security purposes where US involvement is the best geopolitical option—especially to countries that would otherwise be reliant on OPEC or Russia, among others. We saw this very clearly after the Russian invasion of Ukraine and the need for Europe to replace Russian gas. The United States, thankfully, stepped in and is now the largest European supplier of LNG—increasing total export volume by 95 percent from 2019 to 2022.[43]

But the US fossil fuel system as it stands today is completely unsustainable. Our levels of production, imports, exports, associated emissions, and the subsidies that make it all possible will easily blow past Paris Agreement warming limits and lead to a breakdown of our natural climate system. Every positive domestic climate and clean energy action we take is erased by the impact of these other actions. And this was all true before anything President Trump did in his second term.

The Path Forward

Threading a responsible pro-climate needle on current and future energy policy is well within the capability of our elected leaders if we demand it of them. The bottom line is this: if those who say they want energy independence and energy security were truly being genuine, they would move us away from fossil fuels as quickly as possible—an inherently limited system that even fossil fuel companies agree will run out someday, has caused global conflict from the beginning, and is killing us and the planet. They would redirect funds and create a system right here at home that harnesses the unlimited power of the sun, wind, waves, geothermal heat, and nuclear energy.

Even without the political infighting, the intense lobbying from the fossil fuel industries, and the new denialism spreading doubt and fear, we have our work cut out for us. The International Renewable Energy Agency (IRENA) estimates that 90 percent of the world's electricity can and should come from renewable energy by 2050.[44] Not 50 percent, as current projections show, but 90 percent. The remaining 10 percent of various sources of industrial emissions should be offset (reduced to net-zero) through carbon capture and other negative emissions technologies. But this requires the largest physical infrastructure scale-up the world has ever seen and in the shortest imaginable time frame. It also requires much higher levels of investment in new technologies.

The key word here is "can"—the world's electricity can come from renewable and clean energies. Consider that in 2022, about $7 trillion was spent on subsidizing the fossil fuel industry. This number includes explicit subsidies and tax breaks as well as the costs and damages to human health and the environment not directly priced into the cost of fossil fuels.

These human and environmental harms are driving up our costs of food, healthcare, and home insurance. In 2018, the global cost of just air pollution from fossil fuels was $2.9 trillion and contributed to millions of deaths.[45] This will increase over time. A recent study from the Potsdam Institute for Climate Impact Research showed climate change will cost an estimated $38 trillion per year by 2050 due to damages from extreme weather, to infrastructure, food supply, productivity, and health. That could cost each person around 20 percent of their income at that time.[46]

What might redirecting that $7 trillion per year into renewable energy do to accelerate the energy transition? According to the UN, only about $4.5 trillion a year needs to be invested in renewable energy until 2030—including investments in technology and infrastructure—to allow us to reach net-zero emissions by 2050 and avoid catastrophic costs due to a warming world.[47]

Changing all of this may seem daunting. But remember that energy use shifts with hundreds of choices we make from all sectors of the economy. We've explored some ideas that could cause massive shifts, from ending fossil fuel subsidies and redirecting those funds to domestic and affordable renewable energy, to taking a hard look at our oil, gas, and coal production and exports. There are still many more solutions to explore in future chapters. The most important point I hope you take away from these pages is that it will cost us much less to become sustainable than not to.

3

Three Obstacles to Solving Climate Change

Transitioning our global energy structure away from fossil fuels is a complex problem, but it is not, on its own, what stops us from solving climate change. That has much more to do with how we identify, organize, and mobilize. There are three major obstacles standing in the way of our ability to agree upon and implement everything we need to do. All future climate action flows from our ability to overcome them.

The Obstacle of Polarization

Climate change has become one of the most politically polarized issues in the United States, largely due to decades of disinformation and misinformation campaigns attacking climate science, combined with voters sorting into two major parties that stand on opposite ends of the issue. To make matters worse, there is some red herring data that *seemingly* indicate growing support for wide-ranging climate action.

For instance, a survey of nearly 60,000 participants from 63 countries found that 73 percent of people around the world believe "climate change is a serious threat."[1] An even larger survey of more than 73,000 people across 77 countries—the largest ever conducted on climate change—found that 89 percent wanted more government action.[2] Another poll shows at least 70 percent of Americans think global warming is happening and 72 percent think it will harm future generations.[3] Yet another shows 56 percent of Americans say the federal government should do more to reduce the effects of global climate change.[4]

Seems like a positive trend, right? We see the news headlines generated from them that claim "Most Americans" or "Most People Worldwide" support climate action. But when we break these surveys down by partisan affiliation, a different picture emerges, one of clear polarization.

The Pew Research Center has studied Americans' views on climate change for years. In one of their surveys, they ask respondents whether or not climate change is affecting their local community "a great deal" or "some." As of 2023, a majority of Americans (61 percent) say yes to the two categories. But, broken down by partisan affiliation, 84 percent of Democrats agree climate change is affecting their local community a great deal or some, compared to only 36 percent of Republicans.[5] Pew has conducted this survey multiple years, and the numbers have not changed dramatically over time.

For instance, in 2021, it was 57 percent total—still a majority—but with 78 percent of Democrats and just 32 percent of Republicans agreeing.[6] Add in the margin of error and you're seeing movement over time of only a couple points at most. This is despite constant worldwide scientific education, activism, and ever-growing climate damages. People are, sadly, in their ideological camps on the issue of climate change.

I really like Pew's framing. You can find many studies that ask people if they think climate change is a "threat," or if the government, or corporations, or the fossil fuel industry should "take action" or "do more." This typically returns some sort of positive result, if generic and not entirely useful. But, when you get more specific and ask someone, "do you think climate change is impacting your local community"— all of a sudden, the issue becomes real and personal to the respondent and their family. This question strikes at the heart of our developed perceptions and ideologies around the issue and perfectly illustrates some of the reasons behind our polarized views. Pew agrees.

One of the critical findings in their body of work is that partisan affiliation determines perceptions and beliefs about climate change *more strongly* than the local conditions they actually experience. In other words, someone may be directly experiencing wildfire smoke, extended heat waves, repeated "100-year" storms, flooded streets or homes, or other serious impacts made worse by warming—as we know most Americans already are. But by framing a survey from the perspective of "climate change," the majority of Republicans say they see little or no impact in their community. Pew has also found that Democrats are more likely than Republicans to see extreme weather events as connected to climate change.[7]

One of the reasons for this is that partisan affiliation is rooted in identity—how we see ourselves, our place in the world, and what we value. When we discuss solutions to any societal concern, especially policy solutions, people want to know: how will this affect me? They ask, "What will it cost my family?" "What will I have to give up?" A farmer or oil worker might wonder how a given solution will change their livelihood. Someone wary of big government might fear overreach from Washington or the UN. Questions like these reflect the personal and political identities of that person.

Anti-climate campaigns have played upon people's identities to intentionally divide us. When we raise these valid questions and seek more information from a genuine place of concern, misinformation and disinformation campaigns manipulate the answers we receive in ways that sow distrust and stall solutions. For this reason, here and throughout this book, I intentionally use the language "issue of climate change" to distinguish and separate it from the objective scientific reality of the warming climate. This book won't spend time debating climate science, which is a settled fact and has been covered exhaustively by many others. Moreover, I don't believe the data show that disagreements over scientific nuances are where our polarization on this issue comes from. Decades of public education and physical observations have helped the vast majority of us gain at least a baseline scientific understanding of climate change. Instead, I focus on how the issue of climate change has become polarized by effective campaigns that have negatively influenced people's perceptions of the various proposals that have sought to address the issue over time.

So if partisan identities and effective influence campaigns have pushed us into our camps, how do we overcome this?

Using the language of campaigns, let's start by creating a clear definition of the "number" we need to move. The Pew data tell us that a large majority of one partisan affiliation does not see climate change impacting their local communities. Since most voters fall into one of two affiliations in this country, we can effectively categorize half the country as not directly connecting to the issue. Fifty percent, that is our number.

If you think that's high, remember nearly 20 percent of *Democrats* don't think climate change is affecting their local community, along with more than 60 percent of Republicans. The job of any advocate is to make sure what we do is effective. We cannot be effective on any issue that remains so partisan and polarized.

That's not to say half of all Americans believe climate change is a hoax or are unwilling to support *any* climate policies. Chapter 7 will dig further into the different psychological, cultural, and values-based reasons that shape how each of us responds to the issue of climate change. But until we can overcome the polarization attached to the issue of climate change, 50 percent is a useful number. It also helps us frame the gap in what we call "issue identification."

Issue identification is critical to moving anything we care about forward—the foundation upon which any successful campaign or movement is built. There are many different tactics that can increase issue identification, but the bottom line is always this: "Can people see themselves—their lives, their communities, their stories—in that issue?"

Right now, too many people aren't identifying with the issue of climate change and are, instead, defaulting to their polarized partisan identities. This happens on many issues, and understanding where people are is the first step to creating better tactics that can build better campaigns.

Understanding gaps in issue identification and partisan affiliation can also help us challenge misleading claims of "majority support" in surveys, or in the media, when progress is clearly stalled—from gun control to immigration reform and more. To borrow a Capitol Hill term, a "simple majority" isn't going to cut it on a polarized issue. Building a much higher bar of public support is needed—a super majority—and not just within one political party.

Often, greater issue identification is also needed for specific policy proposals—even for people who may support the overall issue. For instance, someone who thinks climate change is a threat and wants the government to take action may not automatically support a carbon tax. When it comes to how we evaluate whether or not we support specific policies, most people tend to want to understand three things: (1) how will this benefit me, (2) how effective will this proposal be in addressing the concern, (3) how much will it cost?

In 2023, the International Monetary Fund studied the relationship between climate concerns and climate-mitigation policies with the stated goal of helping governments increase support for these policies. They conducted surveys of 30,000 respondents across twenty-eight countries and found that more public support is needed to pass climate policies in those countries. This is despite a majority of respondents saying they saw climate change as a threat.[8] The surveys showed significant gaps in people's understanding of how climate impacts affect them, gaps in understanding how certain policy solutions might benefit them, and concerns over costs.

The IMF report is a perfect case study for why greater issue identification is needed on both the overall issue and the specific policies surveyed. Generic majority support was not enough to translate into support for sweeping new policies. Creating more effective communication strategies was identified as key to overcoming the gaps.

Our job for overcoming polarization therefore becomes twofold:

1. Show those who currently do not see it how climate change affects their local community.

2. Communicate to everyone how effective and beneficial specific climate policies would be—both to society and personally. If people view the issue as a threat but don't understand solutions enough to vote for them, we're no better off than we were.

There will always be some who never identify with these efforts. The hard work is never finished on any issue. But we've seen successful campaigns change stubborn minds—today virtually everyone accepts that not wearing a seat belt or smoking can kill you. We need to similarly convince others to see the direct, imminent danger of climate change.

By the way, in the *Bloomberg* article that covered the IMF report, I am featured in the headline image as myself and others protest in front of the White House on Earth Day. Two homemade activist signs are visible in the image: "3° could end this all," and "Climate Justice Now!" These messages are accurate and connect with those who already know and care about the issue. My sign of, "The Climate Crisis is a Human Crisis"—a more universal and connective message—was not visible in the photo. This is one example of how we can create more effective communication strategies in our public awareness and activism efforts. And through our on-the-ground efforts, perhaps even influence the images and messages media sources choose to use to communicate to wider audiences.

The Obstacle of Paralysis

The cousin to polarization is paralysis. We need to engage more people in the issues we care about, but what if they're losing trust in their institutions, as we've seen? Or what if a defeating frustration is taking hold even among many climate and environmental activists who've worked on these issues for a long time, when it becomes clear to them that so many people still don't, or won't, get it?

It's easy to feel overwhelmed by the constant barrage of crises, leaving us anxious, paralyzed, and discouraged or disillusioned by the lack of progress. That frustration breeds apathy—making it feel like real change is impossible. And just like that, we're stuck in a vicious cycle of inaction and despair.

We know that many people, especially young people, are worried about climate change. We know many feel hopeless about stopping it and betrayed by those in power. "Climate anxiety" isn't just a buzzword—it reflects the real pain of disasters, loss, and trauma. It's something I've experienced. We are seeing it in our everyday lives all the time. Again, the data support this. In 2021, nearly one in three Americans experienced a weather disaster.[9] And it's going to get worse as temperatures increase.

All of this can lead to paralysis. And while climate threats affect everyone, younger generations experience and internalize them in a more direct, immediate way. It shapes how we think about our future in inherently different ways than older generations. For those of us who still have fifty or more years ahead, how do we cope?

There is an antidote—at least to the fear. The second half of this book will lay out practical steps to transform anxiety into action. Taking action and making change are powerful tools for empowerment, keeping us optimistic about the future.

An empowered voting bloc that sees their personal connection to the warming world, sees the links to all issues it cares about, and shows up at the polls at record-high levels during the elections that determine our future, is the worst nightmare for those wishing to keep things status quo. Apathy and paralysis are what they *want*, what they are counting on.

These people, institutions, and industries who can't or won't change, who advocate tirelessly against our sustainable future, who deny the science and manipulate public opinion are often the source of our frustrations and paralysis. But we don't need them. Future chapters will show you why. Let's stop wasting our time trying to convince those who won't be convinced and turn instead to methods that target *anyone's* personal interest to get buy-in and results.

The Obstacle of Stale and Ineffective Messaging

It's a hard truth that effectively half the country doesn't feel directly connected to the issue of climate change and doesn't vote on it as a top priority. But the vast majority of people are reachable. If everyone truly saw themselves in the story of the warming world around them, issue identification would be universal, and we would solve climate change. It's that simple. But this relies on the right strategies, tactics, messages, and images. This is where things start to break down.

Many well-intentioned climate activists, authors, journalists, and leaders are stuck in an echo chamber loop of stale, ineffective messaging. They point to all the same polls I've shown but ignore partisan divides or differences in audiences and focus on the unhelpful "most people believe" part. They become condescending, patronizing, or disdainful toward those who disagree with them. They self-righteously double down on the messages that work for them and those like them, even if those messages don't work for others, and they magically wish for the world to be different. Maybe if they just say the same thing enough times, it will become true.

It is not enough for us to wish for things to be different from how they are. It is our responsibility to act; to make the changes we seek. We must build the campaigns that work in the real world and not the ones that only work in our minds.

The reality is we don't need to convince anyone who already cares about climate change to care just a little bit more. We need to get through to a broader, reachable audience and get out of our own way. Too many advocates and activists are focused on the false perception that humanity and nature are pitted against one another in a zero-sum game. Attend any climate protest and you'll see signs and hear slogans along the lines of "stop destroying the Earth."

This is a holdover from the early days of the environmental movement, and I get it. I work every day to try to increase protections for land and marine ecosystems under threat. But climate change is different, and humanity-versus-nature narratives complicate our ability to pursue solutions. How can we, as humans, be expected to solve climate change if nearly everything we do is painted as the problem? Nature-based messages work for me, but they don't work for everyone. We must cast out what we all know are ineffective messages and move into a "Climate Activism 2.0."

This is not to undercut anything that came before us. We need to build upon the great foundation this movement has given us and honor those upon whose shoulders we stand.

In 1962, Rachel Carson's book *Silent Spring* brought environmental pollution from chemical pesticides to the public's attention, influencing generations and sparking the modern environmental movement. A few years later, in 1969, there was a huge oil spill in Santa Barbara, California, and in Ohio, the Cuyahoga River caught on fire due to industrial pollution. This rapid succession of events and growing public awareness led to the first Earth Day in 1970, the creation of the Environmental Protection Agency, and landmark legislation such as the Clean Air Act and the Clean Water Act.

From then until now, a long list of disasters has helped educate the world about the dangers of environmental degradation and contamination, including: India's Bhopal Cyanide Gas Leak in 1984, the discovery of the Antarctic ozone hole in 1985 due to the use of substances like chlorofluorocarbons in aerosols, refrigeration, and air conditioning, the Chernobyl Nuclear Disaster in 1986, the Exxon Valdez oil spill in 1989, the Deepwater Horizon oil spill in 2010, Amazon Rainforest wildfires linked to industrial deforestation in 2019–2020, concern over microplastics, antibiotic overuse in food production, overfishing, toxic "forever chemicals" that show up in our food and water and last for thousands of years, and many more examples that will continue far into the future.

Over this sixty-year period, we learned a tremendous amount from scientists, researchers, environmental authors like Carson, activists, whistleblowers, investigative journalists, documentarians, and many more. We can back up even further to the 1800s and recognize John Muir's trailblazing contributions to public land protections; to Henry David Thoreau's *Walden* or Ralph Waldo Emerson's essay "Nature." In 1804, the Prussian naturalist Alexander von Humboldt wrote in a letter to Thomas Jefferson that "the wants and restless activity of large communities of men gradually despoil the face of the Earth."[10] By 1844, von Humboldt had developed a working hypothesis that humans were affecting the climate in three ways: "through the destruction of forests, through the distribution of water, and through the production of great masses of steam and gas at the industrial centres."[11] He's credited as the first scientist to predict climate change.

Nearly two hundred years of awareness by these visionaries is reflected in the environmental laws and regulations, behavioral changes, and societal shifts of today. It is easy to see how and why the "Save the Planet" mentality started.

But we are also in different territory today. Rapidly rising global temperatures present new challenges. We must continue to advocate for the sustainable use of our resources and the protection of nature. But the images and messages we use to describe the urgency of climate change are different from those used to spread awareness about a toxic chemical substance, the impacts of logging to a forest, or pollution to a river.

Climate Activism 2.0 is not about minimizing the incredible contributions of all those I just listed. It's about recognizing what worked to address the needs we had in the environmental movement over the last two hundred years but also recognizing that different tactics may be needed to address the urgent climate moment we are now in. Images of polar bears and a world on fire aren't winning any new buy-ins.

This holds true even if you agree that we still have many environmental problems yet to solve alongside climate problems, as I do. And even if you agree that the twin crises of global biodiversity loss and global warming are equally important and intertwined, as I do. But look to the complex frameworks of international and domestic laws that regulate these many separate issues to recognize how different the solutions can be. Laws that address microplastics, refrigerants, biodiversity loss, and power plant emissions are each very different. And where policy differs, so too do partisan identities and personal interests.

* * *

Taken together, the three obstacles to solving climate change presented in this chapter—polarization, paralysis, and stale, ineffective messaging—intentionally turn the focus back on the climate advocate and activist. We too have fallen into ideological messaging traps, tired imagery, and stale tactics that can sometimes do more harm than good by *increasing* polarization or, at the very least, not connecting with the audiences we need to reach. Solving climate change does not rest solely with the nonbelievers. There is self-reflection needed by those who care the most.

We are the ones in a position to make change. The goal of any issue campaign is to win, not to be "right" by proving how "wrong" everyone else is. And we very much need to win the campaign on the issue of climate change, which affects the very survival of humanity. We can't afford to stand still. The fossil fuel industries are waging a campaign against us, and so far, they've been winning. They will gladly continue to fill the void left by our inability to break through these obstacles.

If polarization and partisan identities aren't changing much year after year, even as the climate impacts increase in frequency and intensity, if climate change remains at the bottom of the list of issues voters are concerned about, if half to two-thirds of us stay at home during elections, then clearly we need a change in tactics. This is a reality check to those of us who may think we are reaching some sort of tipping point in climate understanding that has the power to break the logjam of long-held partisan identity. We aren't. Or that if we just push hard enough and keep doing exactly what we've been doing, naysayers will eventually see the error of their ways, and we can magically usher in all the climate policies we need. They won't. That's never how it works on any issue. We have more work to do. Let's roll up our sleeves.

4

Mythbusting and Perils of the Blame Game

Time and energy are limited resources—our attention, most of all. Every issue we care about competes with countless other demands, from global events to personal responsibilities. In advocacy, if our efforts divert time, energy, or attention away from real solutions, or if they deepen divisions, we weaken our collective ability to make progress.

We don't know what works until we try. But when the feedback is clear through election results, polling, or reversals of hard-fought victories, we must be willing to adapt, and fast. If we can't align on strategy within our own movement, how can we effectively communicate solutions to others?

Movements are built on myths. These narratives serve a purpose; they connect us to shared histories and identities. The climate and environmental movements are no exception—many of our strategies rest on long-standing beliefs. But not all myths serve us well. Some reinforce ineffective tactics. Others trap us in outdated thinking.

Still, we cling to certain myths—out of habit, deference to those who paved the way, or fear of the unknown. But when these beliefs hold us back, we must be willing to radically reframe how we think and talk about the fight ahead.

Here are three common myths that hold our movement back and undermine our ability to coalesce around solutions.

The Myth of the Personal "Carbon Footprint" and the Climate Activist Blame Game

In the early 2000s, BP, one of the world's largest oil companies, hired public relations firm Ogilvy & Mather to create an ad campaign in which they asked people on the street, "What size is your carbon footprint?" and filmed their responses. In the ad, one woman asks, "How much carbon I produce, is that it?" Text on screen then reads, "we can all do more to emit less" and encourages viewers to go to BP's website to calculate and lower their personal carbon footprint.[1]

This was the birth of the carbon footprint, as we think about it today.

The concept of the "ecological footprint" has been around since the 1990s—which refers to the natural resources needed to offset the impact of human society. But BP's version was a masterstroke of misdirection. In a clever sleight of hand, they co-opted the words and ideas of the sustainability movement, creating a new framework that effectively passed the responsibility of their unsustainable oil and gas operations onto their consumers. Not a corporate crisis, but a personal failing. The subtext was clear: *if only you made better choices,* demanded fewer things, turned your lights off, and stopped traveling, maybe global warming wouldn't be happening.

This level of manipulation from BP and their PR firm was calculated and intentional. By the time their ad came out, they had known and acknowledged the climate risks of burning fossil fuels for decades.[2] Public concern was growing. They were just looking to escape blame.

It worked.

In the decades since, many well-intentioned climate activists have picked up the torch from Big Oil and played into some of the same climate-denier tactics that shift blame and shame from institutional actors onto individual behavior. Core to Greta Thunberg's activism, for instance, is stopping activities in her life that contribute to her carbon footprint—like flying or eating meat. These activists are commendable as they lead by example and do what they think is right to inspire a movement of individual behavioral change. They, alongside the efforts of BP's advertising campaign, have succeeded in making many of us feel bad about our carbon footprints. Meanwhile, fossil fuel extraction continues to expand around the world—our feelings be damned.

But what about the lifestyles of the rich and famous? Surely we are justified in weaponizing personal responsibility against people like Taylor Swift and the "hypocritical environmentalists" Al Gore and Bill Gates, as they fly in private jets around the world?[3]

In January 2025, Oxfam International posted an Instagram reel showing a rich-looking person standing next to a red Ferrari being mock-interviewed. "I'm a wealth architect," he says, and goes on to brag about his trips on private jets. The mock interviewer asks the rich guy, "how does it feel to be part of the one percent impact on the planet?" The interviewer goes on to explain how a short trip on a jet produces more carbon than the average person produces all year, and that "as a one-percenter, you burn through your entire carbon allowance for the entire year in just ten days. It takes someone in the poorest half of the world three years to emit the same." The video ends with the interviewer saying, "The richest one percent are responsible for enough emissions to cause 1.5 million deaths from heat exposure alone," as a skull emoji is flashed on screen.

This video has it all: shame over flying, blame on the rich, incorporating the individual carbon footprint into the idea of a yearly "allowance" that every person on Earth is somehow supposed to know and adhere to in all our decisions. It even assigns a carbon allowance to the poorest people in the world—although, as it points out, it takes them much longer to reach it. And, disturbingly, it includes a claim that the carbon footprints of the rich are directly responsible for millions of deaths with a call to action of #MakeRichPollutersPay—to which someone has commented with three water gun emojis.[4]

It's a powerful video. It channels outrage, lays blame, and dramatizes the scale of inequality. But it also reinforces the same myth it tries to fight: that climate impact is primarily about individual behavior.

There are many videos like this; countless speeches from well-meaning activists who've sworn off modern forms of comfort; many attempts to blame and shame individual actors as somehow the reason why climate change is happening. Luxury lifestyles provide an all-too-easy populist scapegoat for those of us angry about climate change. But these fixations are misdirected.

The average person does not *produce* carbon; or more accurately carbon dioxide (CO_2)—outside of the biological processes of respiration and decomposition that all living things on Earth go through as part of the natural carbon cycle. In the practical sense—in the "what leads to global warming sense"—fossil fuel companies produce CO_2, not people. Our fossil energy infrastructure and institutions of production produce CO_2. Individuals are consumers. We are not the producers of coal, oil, or natural gas. Even as we rely on these things to fuel our lives—driving, flying, heating, and powering our homes, eating—we didn't choose the system.

It is self-defeating to make everyone feel bad about themselves to try to force a theory of behavioral change that won't work anyway. That's not how issue identification is increased. It's not how campaigns are won. No one in the industrialized world is going backward on their standard of living. If that's what the ask is interpreted as, we play right into the hands of the new climate denialism and we fail. These tactics convey little understanding of the issue and what real solutions look like.

Steve Jobs once famously said, "It's not the customer's job to know what they want." Jobs believed that companies that produce things must put themselves in the shoes of their customers to understand their behaviors and frustrations. By doing this, the company can anticipate customers' needs and build products they didn't yet realize they needed—like the highly advanced computer most people around the world now carry in their pockets.

Applying this to sustainability practices, we, the consumers, should not have to pick the "right" or "wrong" option with every choice we make. We don't need to stop flying, we need to switch to advanced biofuels or go completely electric so that aviation is emissions-free. We don't need to stop eating meat; we need to make sure our agricultural system is sustainable and sequesters more carbon than it produces. Every product on the shelf of every supermarket or store we walk into needs to be produced in a way that reduces and reuses materials in its supply chain by all possible means. This process should happen before the product reaches our hands. Our advocacy focus should always and rightly be on the producers, companies, supply chains, and institutional market players.

I understand our system as it is today is unsustainable. So yes, we should all do what we can to minimize our ecological impact as we work to transition the system. I try to live that way myself. But I also recognize that billions of people around the world don't have that luxury of choice and will reach for whatever product or mode of transportation is cheapest as they fulfill their daily needs. I also hold no illusion that changing my individual behavior will make any difference against worldwide greenhouse gas emissions and the footprint of the entire global energy system.

We also can't hold up the poorest half of the world's minimal carbon footprint as somehow the goal we should all strive for. They should be allowed to industrialize just as we did, and they are, rapidly—which increases their energy demands and grows their carbon footprint. But, again, all forms of energy need to be made carbon-free—for all populations. Where's the social media campaign on #CleanIndustrialization? Perhaps not as catchy, but exponentially more important and impactful.

As for the impact of private jets, there are more than 400 million business trips taken in the United States every year. That's over one million people traveling for work every single day, and many of them can't get to where they need to go by bicycle. The median one-way distance for a business trip is 123 miles.[5] There are 45,000 flights per day in the United States. Worldwide, close to half a million people are in the air at any given moment.

Covid gave us an unprecedented glimpse into what shutting down global transportation and associated manufacturing industries would mean for global emissions. In 2020, there was a seventeen percent emissions reduction in the first half of the year.[6] While historic, no serious person believes grinding our economy to a halt and locking ourselves in our homes is how we'll solve climate change. People need to travel to see their families, turn on air conditioners to stay safe during heat waves, turn on lights to study, and use refrigeration to store food and medicine properly. The limited emissions reductions we saw in early 2020 were only achieved by *everyone* stopping their normal lives—not just the richest one percent. And the isolation, fear, and anxiety that it caused had negative consequences that continue to ripple across society years later.

It was also temporary. Even with that short-term reduction, global average temperature continued to increase. We must be able to sustain emissions reductions, and at much higher numbers, while people are still allowed to live and enjoy their lives.

We will not solve climate change by individual behavior alone—try as many might to promote this false concept. Like some sort of purgatorial loop we can't escape from, too many try to convince us that if we had just taken better personal responsibility, we wouldn't be in this mess. But if carbon footprints for individuals at the top of society's structure are false flags, they are even more so for the rest of us.

Large-scale institutional change is the only thing that will solve climate change. Fossil fuel companies know this, which is why they work so hard to keep us blaming each other. Why are we playing into it? The myth of the carbon footprint is exactly what they want us to believe.

I get what organizations like Oxfam are trying to do. Climate change is about inequity. Inequity over which countries and institutions are responsible for emissions and how those least responsible are now experiencing the worst impacts. But even if their campaign works to inspire individual change in some who already support these efforts, it won't change anything with the richest one percent they are targeting, and it won't make a dent in solving climate change.

Individual actions are key to solving climate change from the perspective of engagement, mobilization, and voting. But the more we focus on infighting and individual actions in connection to their contribution to global carbon emissions—and with that (and here's the point) drive up our guilt, shame, and sense of defeat about not doing a better job in our lives to live more sustainably—the more we play into the decades-long efforts of misinformation and disinformation perpetrated by the climate-denier-industrial-complex. At every stage, attempts were made to shift blame away from the fossil fuel industry and institutions of carbon emissions. We must refocus attention on the real institutional drivers of emissions and bad actors who knowingly structured a world at odds with climate stability. We must ditch the individual blame-and-shame game and keep the activism energy and focus where it belongs.

The Myth of Reversing Climate Change

The second common myth many climate activists, politicians, and those in the media get stuck on is the idea that the warming we've already observed is somehow reversible in the near term.

We've all heard the myth that if you throw a frog into hot water, it will immediately jump out, but if you put the frog in room temperature water and slowly increase it to boiling, it will remain in the water until it boils to death. It's false, of course, and terribly cruel to even try, but as an allegory, it offers a fitting analogy for humanity's relationship with the warming climate, at least up to this point. The temperature has gradually increased, and society has collectively sat on the sidelines as the world starts to boil. Indeed, as the UN Secretary-General António Guterres declared during a press conference in July 2023, the era of global warming has ended and "the era of global boiling has arrived."

But maybe there's another lesson in the story of the frog. In hot water, the frog cannot survive on its own. But what if it had a tiny air-conditioned suit on or could construct a whole little world of temperature-controlled systems inside the pot? What if it could adapt and modify the entire natural ecosystem to withstand the slowly boiling water and, maybe after a long enough period of time, figure out ways to stop it from boiling and even cool the water back down? From the perspective of the water, the world nearly boils. From the perspective of the innovative frog, life continues.

This analogy is in no way an attempt to minimize the impact of the warming world nor to make it seem like we shouldn't be decarbonizing as rapidly as we can. But, while humans and nature are experiencing heat-related emergencies on many levels, our current level of warming must not be viewed as *already* the "boiling point" if we are to have any hope for the future.

The Paris Agreement on climate accepts the facts and trajectory of our warming planet and sets a goal of no more than two degrees Celsius of global average temperature increase over pre-industrial levels by the year 2100. The language actually says, "well below 2°C" and to pursue best efforts to limit temperature increase to just 1.5°C, "recognizing that this would significantly reduce the risks and impacts of climate change."[7]

However, we have already warmed 1.3°C on average. 2024 was the first individual year when the temperature crossed the 1.5°C threshold.[8] (It takes years of sustained temperature spikes to become "global average.") The Paris Agreement was adopted more than ten years ago, and in that time, we have not taken all the actions we needed. We have not been able to significantly reduce the risks and impacts of climate change for billions of people.

So, for the purposes of this book, 2°C is used as the climate "disaster point" and the primary goal of the Paris Agreement that we can still realistically work toward staying under by the year 2100. We can still recognize the changes and consequences we should anticipate along the way to this higher threshold, but pragmatically speaking, a lower goal is no longer achievable. Furthermore, targeting a lower goal and rapidly failing to achieve it could easily contribute more to the anxiety, apathy, and paralysis this book seeks to break us out of.

Climate change is simple math: emissions, over time, equals warming. Staying within the 2°C warming limit will be extremely difficult—and will take historic cooperation and societal transformation. Each year that greenhouse gases continue to be emitted at the present industrial scale, temperatures will increase, and we are still years (potentially decades) from full decarbonization.

Furthermore, even if we stopped all emissions *today*, carbon dioxide, the most prevalent of the greenhouse gases, can stay in the atmosphere for one hundred years or longer. The world will continue to warm further, with what is already up there. We must decarbonize at least 80–100 percent by mid-century to allow for this effect and still stay within our end-of-century warming limit. Even more immediately, this means we must decarbonize at least 50 percent by 2030—just a few short years away.

The Paris Agreement takes all these scientific recommendations and timelines into consideration and builds a living and ever-evolving framework for action. Yearly international climate negotiations drive a flywheel effect of greater scientific understanding and awareness, which in turn drives activism and greater pressure on governments to decarbonize faster, which drives new public policies, more evaluations of our progress along the way, and so on. This process is known as the "Ratchet Mechanism," which ensures global ambition increases, or "ratchets up," on a consistent timeline. Collective decarbonization plans put forward by all countries to date do not currently keep us on track to avoid 2°C. But the ratchet mechanism and other tools built into the process will allow us to bend the curve over time as new technological innovations become available and new support for policies is gained.

And despite what some may say, the process has not failed. Experiencing climate change, as detrimental and destructive as it is to our daily lives, does not mean we've failed. The extraordinary progress we're seeing in renewable energy advances and deployment around the world comes from domestic pledges countries made under international climate cooperation goals. Each year, representatives from 196 countries, public and private organizations, entrepreneurs and innovators, scientists and academics, journalists, and members of the public—tens of thousands of people all told—continue to move the ball forward. We are so much further down the road than we were when we first established this process more than thirty years ago. If we caved to the false perception that this process has failed, scrapped the Paris Agreement and started over, we would just wind up building a new process that looked exactly the same and with the same people at the table. These yearly negotiations and frameworks are what *must* occur when trying to bring the world together to cooperate in solving such a great challenge.

This all leads to a practical fact, the acceptance of which is vital to the radical reframing and toolkit the rest of the book provides. We cannot *reverse* the warming we've already seen, at least not in most of our lifetimes. We must abandon that false hope. The only way to reverse today's levels of warming, and only once we've fully turned off the switch of human-caused emissions, is to deploy massive amounts of innovative technologies that suck the emissions out of the air and store them. These are called Negative Emissions Technologies (NETs), or Carbon Dioxide Removal (CDR). Most NETs or CDR ideas being discussed at the time of writing this book haven't been proven or thoroughly researched or tested at scale to know all their potential consequences. We still have many other steps before CDR.

But even in the face of this sobering reality, let me be clear: this is not cause for despair.

We are not fighting for perfection—we are fighting for climate stability and human sustainability, which we can achieve if we meet the goals of the Paris Agreement. It will take all our collective energy to keep warming from exceeding 2°C. It will require optimism to keep this energy up. The boiling point of civilization is still, thankfully, not here. But our perspective needs to shift and allow for *some* unavoidable change even as we work to limit the worst of those changes. While every additional tenth of a degree matters significantly to the climate system and brings with it increasingly serious challenges to our society, the truly terrifying reality of climate change is what happens if and by how much we exceed 2°C.[9] That is when even the frog in his little suit starts to exceed his capability to keep up with the increasingly hot water around him. There is only so much adaptation possible when the world warms so much, so quickly.

The Myth of "Saving the Planet"

In 1992, the United Nations Framework Convention on Climate Change (UNFCCC) was created. This is the treaty from which the Paris Agreement, the Kyoto Protocol, and other important climate agreements were crafted. The text of the UNFCCC begins with "Acknowledging that change in the Earth's climate and its adverse effects are a common concern of humankind," and ends with "... determined to protect the climate system for present and future generations."

As you can see, this landmark climate treaty was created fundamentally with humanity in mind, not just the environment. Of course, we all see the headlines of what warming will mean for the ocean, forests, ice, and other natural systems. It's terrible. But these reports show what could happen to nature if *we* fail to transform *our* industrial practices. This is an entirely human-driven process, and it is up to us to achieve success.

So why, then, does most of the climate movement seem obsessed with "Saving the Planet"?

Messages like these worked to mobilize more than twenty million people into the streets on April 22, 1970, during the first Earth Day. They worked to galvanize public awareness of environmental harms that helped pass many of our early environmental laws. But nearly sixty years of the same call to action has dimmed its resonance. We face new problems today.

If we fail to solve climate change, on a long enough timeline, the Earth will be fine—it literally does not need saving. The climate will slowly stabilize, and new species will return to repair the scars we inflicted. Whether or not we are still around is the big question.

But here's the more important point. We are the only species on the planet with the ability to consciously act on climate change. So even as our current actions lead to a warming world, we must stop seeing humanity as the core problem and start seeing it as the core solution.

Climate and environmental policymaking may sound mostly nature-based by definition. But from the Paris Agreement on down to every federal, state, and local policy we pass, human interest is at the center. We selfishly create the policies that benefit us the most—and that's okay! In fact, policymakers need to do a much better job communicating how their proposals would positively impact us if they wish for them to have any hope of passing in our politically polarized society.

Take the Clean Air and Clean Water Acts, for instance—some of the most powerful environmental laws ever created anywhere in the world. They established standards to clean up America's air and water from widespread air pollutants filling our skies and toxic chemicals leaching into waterways. But why? Because *we* were getting sick. Similarly, the mission of the Environmental Protection Agency is to "protect human health and the environment."

Concern over negative human impacts drives many of our environmental and climate policies, especially those tied to public health. But consider that not all communities experience these impacts in the same way. A study in 2021 showed that urban extreme heat exposure had increased nearly 200 percent over the past four decades, with a disproportionate impact on low-income communities that don't have the same level of shade/tree canopy and air conditioning as more affluent communities.[10]

You might also consider the term "energy burden"—the percentage of your income that goes toward the cost of heating, cooling, and/or transportation. While higher costs strain anyone's wallet, lower-income and vulnerable populations have much higher energy burdens due to the higher percentage of their income needed to cover their utility bills. This also makes them more at risk from sudden spikes that can increase their household costs—which severe temperatures driven by climate change can certainly bring.

There are many other examples of climate and environmental inequities across the country and world that highlight the need for policies that, yes, protect nature, but also protect and improve our lives. As we work to build more personally relevant connections to more people, the fight to save ourselves, not just the planet, is not only an effective reframing, it's essential.

If we are to achieve the goals of the Paris Agreement and the United Nations Framework Convention on Climate Change more broadly, we will need to protect humanity as much as nature. Just as parents on a plane are expected to put their oxygen masks on first before assisting their children, if we wish to save the planet, we must first save ourselves.

* * *

Addressing and busting the myths of the personal carbon footprint, of reversing climate change, and of saving the planet serves multiple purposes. It helps keep us, as activists and advocates, focused on the solutions that will make the biggest difference. It helps us find better ways of talking to and connecting with people, rather than making them feel scolded or bad about themselves. It provides more optimism that it's not too late to still make a difference and that our plans in place, like the Paris Agreement, are moving us in the right direction. And it removes potential points of conflict and confusion in our messages and tactics.

There are new myths we can build our movement on. We can think about humanity's potentially endless sustainable future and all we might achieve. Of living in harmony with the natural world for the first time in all of human history. Or, yes, of "saving" nature and stopping the catastrophic biodiversity loss we are currently seeing. But by busting the unhelpful myths that hold us back, we can ensure every molecule of public awareness and political traction we gain through our efforts is harnessed toward actions that will actually solve climate change. In today's crowded competition for our attention, we can't afford to squander anyone's time or energy.

Interlude
From Anger to Agency

As we move to the solutions half of this book, I want to spend a moment on what I mean by "solutions." The previous chapters introduced some ideas that could have big impacts—from eliminating fossil fuel subsidies to taking a hard look at US energy imports, exports, and domestic production. What are some others that can help us decarbonize and stabilize the climate?

Project Drawdown, an organization that provides excellent resources on this topic, has identified ninety-three technologies and practices that can reduce greenhouse gases across all sectors. Everything from building more bicycle infrastructure to improving cattle feed, wetlands restoration, and many ideas in between. They have created, as they like to say, "The Most Comprehensive Plan Ever Proposed to Reverse Global Warming."

There are additional sources of comprehensive climate plans. UN agencies have published many of them. There's the Green New Deal. There are "101 Ways to Save the Planet" books and off-the-wall daily calendars that give advice on lowering your carbon footprint (you know how I feel about those).

There was the 538-page report "Solving the Climate Crisis: The Congressional Action Plan for a Clean Energy Economy and a Healthy, Resilient, and Just America," released in 2020.[1] This was heralded in the media as the "most detailed and well-thought-out plan for addressing climate change that has ever been a part of US politics."[2] It stemmed from the House Select Committee on the Climate Crisis—created by Democratic members of Congress and their staff who took climate change seriously and sought to create a comprehensive framework for congressional action. (The committee was terminated by Republicans after they won control of the House in the 2022 midterms.)

Some of these plans have been successful. Hundreds of recommendations made by the House Select Committee on the Climate Crisis made their way into the Inflation Reduction Act, Bipartisan Infrastructure Law, and CHIPS and Science Act. But many others have not. Meanwhile, climate impacts continue to grow. My point is there is no shortage of "plans." But "the best-laid plans of mice and men often go awry," as they say.

This is, in part, due to a public misunderstanding of what effective climate solutions look like. We must move beyond the mindset of "doing something" about climate change that we're currently stuck in and that leads to mostly reactionary, incremental, and too-slow progress. We must move into the new frame of, "what does it look like for us to actually *solve* climate change?"

This is a fundamental distinction that is often lost in the national climate conversation. It requires a clear vision for what success looks like. In presenting solutions, I highlight additional examples of some of the best ideas I think would have a huge impact. But I won't recreate the exhaustive work of so many. Rather, my solutions are designed to build *support* for all the painstakingly researched and thought-out plans we've already put forward but have failed to fully implement so far.

Key to building this support is a radical reframing of how we *think* and *talk* about climate change—which Chapters 5 through 7 will do. I use these simple concepts to make clear how all the problems from the first half of this book lead us into two frameworks for solutions that are easy to understand and critical to follow. New images, messages, and tactics are introduced that challenge preconceptions about what "climate" or "environmental" messages are "supposed" to sound and feel like.

But I begin this reframing with our next chapter on mitigation and adaptation. Specific examples of damages from rising temperatures are included. Elevating stories of individual impact from the warming world is key to building more personal and community-level connections to the issue. But we don't just want to list an endless litany of how bad everything is. There are many sources of terrible news related to how climate change is increasingly ravaging our world. Most exclude a detailed analysis of how we should understand these negative impacts and what we can do, if anything, to solve them.

For example, is this wildfire I'm reading about something that could have been prevented, or will it become the new normal my community is supposed to adapt to? How do I think about the loss of life from this major flood—is there anything we can do to improve infrastructure to deal with future floods? Would a reduction of greenhouse gas emissions have reduced any of these impacts?

The next chapter still presents many problems we need to solve. But it also bridges into solutions by presenting new ways to think and talk about climate damages that can enable us to more effectively address them. I use the terms of mitigation and adaptation in more personal ways so you may understand your role in the changing world more directly and now, not in the future. This is critical to reframing the issue of climate change.

The final three chapters put our reframings to work in action steps and how-to guides for engagement in combating climate change in your life, your community, and at all levels of government. My solutions provide a template for understanding climate impacts on a deeper, more realistic, and more personal level while also critiquing what has worked and what hasn't on other issue efforts. They build a clear outline of the work we still must do to achieve success. They show how turning anger into agency and action starts with helping people see themselves in the fight.

Let's dive in.

5

Mitigation, Adaptation, Loss, and Damage

For the last few decades, experts have used two main categories to sort everything related to the actions we can take to address climate change into—*mitigation* and *adaptation*. The United Nations defines climate mitigation as "human interventions to reduce the emissions of greenhouse gases by sources or enhance their removal from the atmosphere by 'sinks'. A 'sink' refers to forests, vegetation or soils that can reabsorb CO_2."[1] This can mean transitioning away from fossil fuels and deploying new clean energies, or reducing energy demand through increased efficiency in anything from industrial practices to home appliances. A regulation that improves the fuel efficiency of cars to 58 miles per gallon, for instance, is a policy that "mitigates" the emissions from vehicles and their warming impact on the climate. A large-scale reforestation campaign would be an example of mitigating emissions by enhancing the carbon sink.

Adaptation, on the other hand, is defined as "adjustments in ecological, social or economic systems in response to actual or expected climatic stimuli and their effects."[2] Building a flood barrier or seawall, installing cooling centers in urban areas for vulnerable populations during a heatwave, adopting stricter building codes, and improving water usage and storage in fire-prone areas are all adaptive actions to climate impacts.

Until recently, the conversation around climate policy solutions has mostly focused on mitigation. The success of our efforts to mitigate greenhouse gas emissions will determine whether or not we exceed critical temperature thresholds. If we do, many of our adaptation needs may become insurmountable.[3] So mitigation policies are, rightly, the primary tools to avoid this disaster point. They're also more cost-effective. The higher the temperature rises, the more expensive adaptation becomes. Investing in mitigation early, like compound interest in one's retirement account, yields an increasingly higher return on investment relative to high adaptation costs later. Therefore, if you have one billion dollars of public sector funds to spend on climate solutions today, spend it on projects that *reduce* carbon emissions so that you don't have to spend ten billion dollars ten years from now trying to *adapt* to the consequences.

But a focus on adaptation has been growing alongside mitigation, as the world warms and impacts grow more severe. We can no longer avoid the large-scale adaptation investments we need to safeguard us against the warming we're already experiencing. These are big public works projects and associated policies that would secure their funding, such as: restoring coastal ecosystems that act as a buffer against hurricane storm surge, upgrading pipes and drainage systems, and installing heat-resistant roofs and roads. The Green Climate Fund, for instance, one of the main banks for international climate development in developing countries, is already committed to a 50:50

balance between mitigation and adaptation in its lending portfolio. Unfortunately, world leaders have been slow to commit the necessary funds to either category at the scale and timeline required.

Resilience: Reflecting the New Reality

As needs grow, how we think about mitigation and adaptation must also evolve. In some circles, it has. Mitigation is now understood by those on the front lines of infrastructure planning as efforts that can reduce or prevent the effects *of natural hazards*—like a large storm, heatwave, flood, or fire. A 2019 report from the National Institute of Building Sciences found that $7 in avoided losses are saved for every $1 of public funds invested in riverine-flood mitigation.[4] A 2024 report from the US Chamber of Commerce found that $13 in economic costs, damages, and cleanup are saved for every $1 invested in disaster preparation. The Chamber also reported that, in 2022 alone, natural disasters around the world cost more than $360 billion.[5] Both organizations acknowledge they are likely underestimating both their benefit and cost numbers as preparing for and effectively mitigating hazards has far greater value than can easily be modeled, while failure to do so causes permanent harm that extends well beyond the cleanup.

Mitigation in this sense is about building resilience against climate impacts—flood resilience, fire resilience, coastal resilience, and so on. Or, coming at it from the adaptation side, resilience can be thought of as the sum of all adaptive actions. In other words, has our adaptation planning created a resilient system that can withstand these hazards?

Resilience is a simpler way to understand how the categories of mitigation and adaptation combine into real-world implications for people where they live and today. Building resilience to climate change, extreme weather, or other naturally occurring disasters *should* be viewed as common sense by policymakers. And it's desperately needed.

* * *

Let's remove all the buzzwords and ask a simple question: How safe are we from the impacts of climate change in the places we live?

The Intergovernmental Panel on Climate Change (IPCC) is "the United Nations body for assessing the science related to climate change." Its objective is "to provide governments at all levels with scientific information that they can use to develop climate policies."[6] In 2022, the IPCC released a report assessing human vulnerability to climate risks. Some of its key findings were condensed into a fact sheet, which stated: "Many cities and settlements have developed adaptation plans, but few have been implemented, so that urban adaptation gaps exist in all world regions and for all hazard types. Current adaptation is unable to resolve risks to current climate change associated hazards."[7]

Translation: we are not prepared. No town, Democratic or Republican, urban or rural, rich or poor, is ready for the climate changes we are already seeing.

I've protested in our nation's capital for climate change, racial justice, civil rights, and more. With the White House or Capitol building as the backdrop, calls for action emanating from the crowd always feel powerful. If enough marching feet come together, it seems, the federal government must listen—it must hear the people's calls behind their white pillars. Every April for Earth Day, activists around the world come together to protest environmental crises. I've stood in those crowds, holding signs demanding we "fight for our future."

But when I first read this IPCC report, something shifted. A march about general climate awareness, international action, or federal government action isn't going to cut it. We know the problem; we've signed the international agreements, we have the government's attention—well, at least some people in government. But now we know the scope of vulnerability to the very streets of the cities we'll be marching through.

Nowhere is safe. Climate change has become local.

For example, Washington, DC, where many of these marches take place—with its Democratic majority and highly engaged citizenry—is not immune to climate vulnerability. Flooding from rising seas threatens the city as tidal rivers swell their banks during heavy rainfall.[8] In extreme weather, storm surge from the Potomac to the Anacostia could pour through the National Mall.[9] This risk is imminent enough that a flood barrier has already been installed capable of holding back up to nineteen feet of water from destroying some of DC's most iconic buildings.[10]

DC is also getting hotter. Some neighborhoods are reaching a life-threatening heat index of 115 degrees Fahrenheit in the summers, with little ability for many low-income residents in those neighborhoods to cool off even at night, given the high humidity and lack of access to air conditioning.[11] This is a trend observed all over the world. A 2021 study showed that urban extreme heat exposure had increased nearly 200 percent over the past four decades, with a disproportionate impact on low-income communities.[12]

Projects that build resilience to flooding and extreme heat can mitigate these negative climate impacts across DC's residents. By definition, these are also adaptive actions. But I think you can see how much more personal and community-specific the language of resilience can be.

Dual-Benefit

Resilience brings mitigation and adaptation together into a framework that reflects the needs of the warming world. This can also be thought of as "dual-benefit." Sustainable agriculture, for example, is dual-benefit. It has the potential to suck greenhouse gases out of the air and sequester them in crops and soil (mitigation) while also employing sustainable land-use policies that can build resilience against pests, drought, flood, and other impacts that could devastate other types of farmland (adaptation).

Another example: a federal stimulus bill that invests billions in industrial manufacturing facilities that create jobs across the country while also making these facilities more energy efficient (mitigation), powered by decentralized renewable energy so the lights stay on in a major storm (adaptation), and transports all their products using a fleet of EV delivery vehicles (mitigation again). These are examples of resilient systems that use mitigation and adaptation strategies to return dual climate benefits as well as jobs and economic benefits.

We should think of all climate investments—whether for infrastructure or disaster planning, adaptation or mitigation—as part of a single category: building national and local resilience. This framing makes it easy to show lots of additional co-benefits people care about. It also meets people where they are with what they're experiencing in their lives and communities. Policy proposals and climate plans that don't reflect this on-the-ground application are doomed, never to gain the political buy-in necessary to translate into real-world action.

As then–Speaker of the House Nancy Pelosi said of the landmark 2020 report by the House Select Committee on the Climate Crisis, it "was not intended to be just an academic endeavor, but to guide major climate legislation across the committees to make informed recommendations and deliver on our moral obligation to children and future generations."[13] This pragmatic framing, focused on positive public reception and impactful outcomes, is how, as stated, hundreds of recommendations laid out by the committee made it into the Inflation Reduction Act, Bipartisan Infrastructure Law, and the CHIPS and Science Act. Collectively, these three pieces of legislation enabled us to take giant steps forward in our ability to build climate resilience across our country.

Loss and Damage

There is one more category of understanding climate impacts, actions, and solutions that is rapidly—and unfortunately—gaining in importance. These are the losses and damages incurred by nature and people that go *beyond* natural climate variability. This is the category of climate impacts we won't be able to mitigate, adapt to, or build resilience to in time.

Loss and damage isn't a new idea. It's been debated for decades, and the two words are viewed distinctly by advocates. "Loss" is clear and includes economic and non-economic losses like the loss of ancestral burial grounds, an entire culture, language, or country—which may happen to some island nations as sea levels rise. The loss of life or livelihood. The extinction of a species. I know this sounds grim, but given its extreme impact (particularly in the developing world), this is where some of the highest levels of energy and momentum are among climate activists, particularly with young people who are looking for hands-on ways to mobilize their affected communities.

"Damage," on the other hand, assigns costs to these losses and seeks liability. Advocates think about this from a legal perspective and strive to assign responsibility to countries most responsible for creating damages—like the United States and our emissions. This is what scares climate negotiators from the industrialized world and why progress on addressing loss and damage has been slow. Once individual countries start accepting blame, there might be no end to the financial damages sought against them.

The Paris Agreement recognizes loss and damage but not liability and compensation. The 2022 UN climate conference in Sharm el-Sheikh, Egypt—"COP27"—culminated with the creation of a new Loss and Damage fund. This was years in the making and a great first step for the developing nations that desperately need help. But there is still a lot of uncertainty about how this fund differs from other mitigation and adaptation funds already in need of investment. This will be an important space to watch, especially as climate losses build.

Courtney Durham Shane is an international climate policy expert who has attended twelve UN climate conferences (and counting).

She is also a friend and colleague. Courtney has been part of international climate finance conversations that seek to gain more funds for mitigation and adaptation, part of efforts to create new strategies for resilience planning and clean energy deployments in communities across the United States, and has followed loss and damage negotiations firsthand. I asked her how she makes sense of all the categories of climate impacts and solutions, and how we can make it more personal. Here's what she told me:

> We didn't leave the Stone Age because we ran out of stones. We entered the Bronze Age because there was a better path. We don't have to wait until fossil fuels completely run out before we think about what a clean energy transition looks like. All climate policies have associated costs and parallel benefits. We can weave a positive economic narrative into all of this. But as we talk about what is good for the economy we must also talk about what is equitable. Many young people want a clean economy but they don't want investments that will continue to perpetuate inequalities in the same way the fossil fuel system has for hundreds of years. We have to be careful that the incredible wealth being generated in this new economic driver doesn't perpetuate deep inequities that we've seen in the industrial and fossil fuel eras.

* * *

Every town and city in every part of the world is experiencing some degree of loss and damage right now, as the IPCC report shows in its analysis of adaptation gaps. Let's review a few major events that have happened just since I started writing this book. We will then try to understand how these and similar events in the future may be better addressed using the tools of mitigation, adaptation, and/or resilience.

The summer of 2023 turned into a weird, orange hellscape for many of us: smoke from hundreds of out-of-control wildfires hundreds of miles away burned an area twice the size of Switzerland. Daily changes in wind patterns were the only reprieve from dangerous air quality for 120 million people from the Midwest to New England. Hundreds of millions of Americans were threatened by the very air outside their windows, by a failure of the system. At the same time, 100 million *more* Americans faced extreme and unrelenting heat in the West and Gulf—just one electricity grid failure away from a public health nightmare.

In 2024, we had the earliest catastrophic hurricane (Beryl) pass through—the only June Category 4 on record in the Atlantic Ocean. At the same time, half the country, around 162 million people, experienced an extended record-breaking heat wave. Las Vegas, for example, recorded an all-time high of 120 degrees. Even more deadly was the combination of these two things at once. Hurricane Beryl left three million people in Texas without power for days during a heat wave upwards of 110°F. Different climate hazards can happen concurrently and compound their impacts on humanity. By the end of this century, some tropical coastal areas could face up to six simultaneous hazards.[14]

Anyone with a phone now gets what seems like nonstop notifications every summer about "Excessive Heat Warnings" with "significant threat to life or property." Many of us remember when extreme weather was less than a daily occurrence. And we aren't just more sensitive today. A heat index of 110° F is truly a significant threat. A 2023 study showed that if an extended electricity grid failure occurred in Phoenix during a heat wave for more than a few days, 12,800 people could die and 800,000 more could need hospitalization. This would overwhelm the local hospital system, which only has 3,000 ER beds.[15] In fact, that many people would overwhelm the entire nation's hospital system.

Don't believe me? Consider this. At the height of the pandemic, around 160,000 people were hospitalized for Covid at any given time—and we all followed the news of how close we came to overwhelming ERs and ICUs. What excessive heat could do to just one unprepared city, and how that could reverberate across the entire country, is truly daunting. And, as with any extreme climate impacts, vulnerable populations suffer the most.

From 1961 to 2023, the heatwave frequency, intensity, duration, and length of the season all increased dramatically in the fifty US urban areas that were studied. Whereas two heatwaves would once hit major US cities per year on average, now there are six. The average heatwave season is forty-six days longer now than it was in the 1960s. This data adjusts for what is considered "normal" in terms of local conditions. Some cities are located in places that have always been hot. But now, they are hotter in a significantly "unusual" way.[16]

Let me make this even more personal.

I live in the Shenandoah Valley of Virginia's Blue Ridge Mountains. I've attended the Appalachian Trail Days celebration in Damascus several times and hiked all over southwestern Virginia. My trips to Asheville have blown me away with how fun that mountain city is. Boone, North Carolina, along the Blue Ridge Parkway, is one of the most beautiful places I've ever seen in autumn. Grandfather Mountain

State Park, Linville Gorge Wilderness, and Blowing Rock. The small towns in western North Carolina are remote, beautiful, and filled with amazing music, food, art, and people.

This region was devastated by Hurricane Helene in late September 2024. It will take years to fully recover—and many of the small towns had underdeveloped infrastructure to begin with. The loss of life stands alone and cannot be recovered. But the economic losses compound things even further, as the hurricane hit right before peak fall tourism season—one of the busiest and most important times of year for businesses and residents in that area.

Hurricane Helene made landfall in Florida, not North Carolina or Virginia. It was the strongest hurricane on record to strike Florida's Big Bend region. Unusually warm Gulf waters—among the hottest recorded—fueled rapid intensification, transforming Helene from Category 1 to Category 4 in just 16 hours. But then Helene collided with another run-of-the-mill rain system already hitting southern Appalachia, supercharged it, and dumped 20 trillion gallons of rain on the Southeast US over the course of one week. Catastrophic flooding, the worst on record in the region, followed.

I saw the aftermath of Hurricane Katrina in 2005 firsthand, another storm worsened by warming waters. Katrina first hit Florida as a Category 1, then crossed the state to the Gulf of Mexico where it rapidly intensified to a Category 5. It made landfall again in Louisiana as a Category 3 and then *again* in Mississippi.[17] The warming waters also made the storm surge worse. Studies show Katrina's flood elevation was 15–60 percent higher than it would have been under the climate conditions 100 years prior, with clear links shown between rising global temperatures, rising sea levels, and higher flood elevations.[18]

The sheer size and scale of Helene reminded me of Katrina. In fact, Helene was the deadliest hurricane to strike the mainland United States since Katrina. But while Katrina devastated coastal regions, Helene did its worst damage hundreds of miles inland, in the mountains.

I also have family in Los Angeles. The January 2025 fires terrified us as we worried for their safety. And California—thanks to progressive climate policies, public support for increased regulation, a high tax base that can afford big infrastructure projects, and some of the best and well-trained firefighters in the world—is one of the most climate-prepared places anywhere. And yet, *six* concurrent fires hitting the second-largest US city overwhelmed their system.

We are seeing a return of a type of fire that once plagued cities but was thought to be mostly extinct in the modern era—the "urban conflagration." Think of the Great Chicago Fire of 1871 or the San Francisco Earthquake and Fire of 1906. A century ago, mostly wood-built cities without fire codes or flame-retardant building materials experienced catastrophic fires much more than they do today. But now, wildfires ignited on the edge of urban areas are turning into conflagrations once again. Even though these fires start in the zone of transition between forests (or otherwise unoccupied natural lands) and human development—referred to as the Wildland-Urban Interface or WUI (pronounced "woo-ie")—conflagrations are *not* a wildfire-driven problem. The fire becomes something different once it hits dense urban areas. Driven once again by climate change that creates severe drought conditions and higher wind intensity, conflagrations burn in vastly different environments than wildfires—feeding on very little vegetation but instead jumping from building to building and ripping through entire neighborhoods. Los Angeles was an example of this, as was Lahaina, Hawaii in 2023.[19] There will be more.

I could go on as, I'm sure, you can too. These examples from just the last few years add to a growing list of severe climate impacts already hitting the places we live. These are not future threats—they're happening now. And we are not prepared. To solve climate change in this regard, we need policies that mitigate risk, prepare for disaster, and rebuild after inevitable damages. And, of course, we must reduce emissions to avoid the even worse impacts of the much hotter world we will see if we don't transition away from fossil fuels.

Turning Impact into Action

Each example of climate impacts happening close to home, while terrifying, also adds to our ability to raise public concern and calls for action—if the right framework for understanding them is put in place. The first step is to get really specific about what happened and the tools we need to be more effective in the future. Use the language we have established and that people respond to: how will this benefit me; how effective will this proposal be in addressing the concern; how much will it cost? Only after this practical framework has been established should we try to connect these events to climate change. Immediately framing every new storm or extreme weather event from a climate lens runs the risk of polarizing people and slowing our ability to agree upon clear mitigation and prevention solutions. We know Republicans are less likely to see extreme weather events as connected to climate change.[20] Weather is not climate, and not all weather-related disasters are related to climate change.

Each disaster highlighted in this chapter *was* made worse by climate change, and I showed how. But they also show how limiting it can be to try to understand what is happening only through a "climate" or "environmental" lens—which is why I included specific details about the losses and damages to people and local economies. Issue identification is only increased if people understand these specifics. But once they do, these traumas in our collective national memories can empower us to force the leaders of the places we live to step up— to protect us and build resilience in places like Damascus, Asheville, Boone, Waveland, Los Angeles, Las Vegas, Phoenix, Houston, Lahaina, and everywhere else. We can help get them there.

Of course, not everything can be solved locally. But turning impact into action and better managing climate risks at the local level also helps limit the federal government's fiscal exposure when severe examples of loss and damage require federal assistance. The Government Accountability Office (GAO) has been studying this for years. They've found that the effects of climate change have already cost the federal government many billions of dollars, and those costs will increase. Taking steps to enhance climate resilience won't eliminate these costs, but they can significantly reduce them over time compared to doing nothing—which also reduces our burden as taxpayers.

Unfortunately, GAO found the federal government is currently not well-positioned to manage the growing climate impacts and associated costs. In 2023, the United States sustained twenty-eight climate-related weather events and natural disasters that cost over $1 billion each and resulted in $94.1 billion in total damages. In 2024, there were twenty-seven disasters with at least $1 billion in economic damages each. In GAO's own words, the "frequency and intensity [of these disasters] have severely strained the Federal Emergency Management Agency (FEMA) and its workforce," among other agencies.[21]

The ballooning costs of fighting forest fires are already overwhelming the annual budget and capacity of the United States Forest Service. And, over the next few decades, tens of billions of additional dollars may be needed in federal funding for hurricane disaster response.

This is unsustainable, even at current climate-impact levels. Alongside local action, GAO recommends that Congress act to organize the federal government to prioritize climate resilience, better manage climate risk, and improve its ability to provide disaster assistance when needed. For instance, the Department of Housing and Urban Development (HUD) now manages the federal government's largest investment in disaster recovery and resilience planning in low-to-moderate-income communities across the country. But higher levels of investment are needed to keep up with growing risks to human health and safety driven by climate change.[22]

The increase in disasters also severely strains state budgets. For example, in Washington state, the average budget costs associated with fighting wildfires tripled from around $24 million per year in 2014 to $83 million per year in 2019.[23] In many states, fire suppression and other efforts are now exceeding state budgets. Compounding this, not enough funds are being allocated toward programs that would help mitigate future risk, so states are having to spend far more on disaster recovery and response than they would have if they had invested more in mitigation.

Despite the work we still have to do, there are positive examples of state and local resilience planning. As of July 2023, twenty-one states had created an office to deal with the broad range of impacts related to natural disasters and their costs.[24] This is usually known as a "resiliency office," which is led by a "Chief Resilience Officer" (CRO). In West Virginia, for instance, all of the state's fifty-five counties are at risk of flooding.[25] According to the National Flood Insurance Program, just one inch of flooding can cause upwards of $25,000 in damages to a home.[26] Yet, homeowners' and renters' insurance policies typically do not cover flood damage. These and other "Act of God" events—as insurance companies like to call them—are typically defined as "an unpreventable and destructive event that is caused by nature."[27] So the mission of the West Virginia Chief Resilience Officer is to "minimize the loss of life and property, maintain economic stability, and improve recovery time by coordinating with stakeholders to implement disaster resilient strategies."[28]

CROs can help their states, counties, and cities coordinate responses and implement plans to deal with flooding, fire, heat, and other impacts from climate change. This can be a major step in getting state and local leaders to reduce the risks from any disaster—climate-related or otherwise. Common sense strategies to deal with natural disasters, again, *should* be welcomed by most people, regardless of their ideologies. And it's a big part of how we make the places we live more resilient to climate change, whether or not everyone in those places believes climate change is real or affecting them. I firmly believe we can cut through partisan identities with programs that help keep us safe.

In summary, it's worth repeating that framing these programs from the perspective of "disaster resilience" and not necessarily "climate change" helps make them more accepted in both the Democratic and Republican states in which they've been created. And as rising temperatures bring with them many more acts of God, any work we can do to help people be better prepared is worth it.

6

Reframing How We Think about Climate Change

Life and Love

In the late 1980s, an anti-abortion campaign named "Operation Rescue" was launched with the slogan "if you believe abortion is murder, act like it's murder." Tactics included rallying outside abortion clinics, harassing workers and women who sought services, blocking access, and other forms of intimidation and civil disobedience that led to tens of thousands of arrests. The Southern Poverty Law Center lists terror, militancy, and violence as some of the most effective weapons of the anti-abortion movement over time. Since 1977, anti-abortion activists have committed 11 murders, 42 bombings, 200 acts of arson, and 531 assaults—which were all directed at patients or those working in abortion care.[1]

These extreme and violent tactics led to the decline of Operation Rescue throughout the 1990s. They were also largely ineffective.

Clinics learned how to deal with protestors, court cases ruled against them, and federal legislation made it a federal crime to "physically obstruct or use violence or the threat of violence to prevent someone from obtaining reproductive health care services." Abortion services continued.

At the same time, however, the message of "pro-life" gained traction. Many in the movement used this pro-life frame to broaden their appeal. Who can be against life? Life is not a "choice"—responding to the message of pro-choice. As they saw it, life is God-given, and they were fighting to save lives.

To the extent this movement has now "won," with *Roe v. Wade* overturned in 2022, this is the frame they won on. They also very effectively pivoted to state and local policy changes and legal system challenges as they built public support. Abortion access is no longer federally protected. At the time of writing this book, twelve states have total abortion bans, and twenty-nine more have bans based on gestational limits.[2]

The marriage-equality movement faced similar pivot points in the early 2000s. The Defense of Marriage Act prevented the federal government from recognizing same-sex marriages. Angry protesters (rightly) railed against a system that discriminated against them. States passed civil union laws that granted rights to same-sex couples but from a technical, administrative perspective. Leading advocates like Evan Wolfson and others in the Freedom to Marry movement won majority support for gay marriage in some places, but then ballot measures and other opposition efforts peeled those wins back. The movement needed to reach beyond their initial supporters and into the next category of people they could persuade to build lasting change.

It wasn't enough to focus on rights and legal benefits—they needed a message that could connect emotionally across belief systems and political identities. Freedom to Marry recalibrated their message to focus on empathy and shared values. Their message became: "Love is Love."

People, no matter who they are or what they believe, get married because they love each other. They build a family out of love. Love is a universal value anyone can identify with. This message helped to reach more people—solidifying the state-based marriage equality wins. This culminated in 2015 when the Supreme Court guaranteed the fundamental right to marry to same-sex couples under the Due Process Clause and the Equal Protection Clause of the Fourteenth Amendment.

* * *

These successful campaign examples and others were highlighted for me in conversation with Leslie Crutchfield, Executive Director of the organization Business for Impact at Georgetown University's McDonough School of Business. Leslie includes these case studies in her 2018 book *How Change Happens: Why Some Social Movements Succeed While Others Don't*. She also profiles anti-tobacco campaigns, Mothers Against Drunk Driving, and the success of gun rights activists. As she explained to me,

> successful movements are intentional and deliberate about how they attempt to reframe how their target audience thinks about the cause. Many movements overlook this. They instead start with the frame of "we're right, we have the facts and the science on our

side—people should just agree with us." But that's not how we motivate people. You have to communicate in emotional, visceral ways to engage with your supporters, your allies, your members. Honey catches more flies than vinegar.

That's what both the anti-abortion and marriage-equality movements learned to do and how, after many years of setbacks, they both finally won. "Life" and "Love" reframed how people thought about each of those issues and expanded their bases of support.

Leslie also strongly believes in the power of grassroots movements, as do I. These campaigns could not have won without on-the-ground engagement from people all over the country coming together in a shared sense of purpose. People advocating for these issues lived in the same town, worshipped together, went to the same bars, and their kids played in the same sports leagues. Once you find the right message to bring your target audience together—and build that grassroots infrastructure within communities—you can build a successful movement that leads to national change.

You also have to study your opposition. In the fights for marriage equality and against abortion, there was no group, no powerful industry profiting from the status quo. These were religious, cultural, and moral battles, and they had to be waged with messaging and tactics that reflected them. The climate change battle is different. It presents a deeper, more complex challenge as entrenched economic interests have a direct stake in preventing progress. But even so, narrative has power. You can reframe the story or stories in a way that changes hearts, shifts worldviews, and galvanizes more people.

The right messages—anchored in values people already hold—can cut through profit-driven resistance and ignite a movement.

Climate Change Means . . .

In Dr. Frank Luntz's 2008 book *Words that Work: It's Not What You Say, It's What People Hear*, he lists "Ask a Question" as one of his ten rules of effective language. Think of the immensely popular "Got Milk?" advertising campaign or Verizon Wireless's "Can you hear me now?" slogan. "The reason for the effectiveness of questions in communication is quite obvious," Luntz states. "When you assert, whether in politics, business, or day-to-day life, the reaction of the listener depends to some degree on his or her opinion of the speaker. But making the same statement in the form of a rhetorical question makes the reaction personal—and personalized communication is the best communication."

Luntz credits his rule to Democratic media consultant Tony Schwartz and his "Responsive Cord" theory of communication.[3] Luntz describes Schwartz's theory and his own interpretation of it as "people [react] best to language and messages that [are] participatory—allowing the receiver to interact with the message and the messenger."[4]

If you think my mentioning the name Frank Luntz in a book about climate change is odd, perhaps even offensive, you would not be alone. Luntz is a renowned Republican pollster, communications expert, and political strategist. He has shaped conservative messaging over decades, from helping to create Newt Gingrich's "Contract with America" to reframing the snoringly boring term "estate tax" into the scary-sounding "death tax." He advised President George Bush and the Republican Party in the early 2000s to stop using the term "global warming" and instead use "climate change" because, as he wrote, "while global warming has catastrophic communications attached to it, climate change sounds a more controllable and less emotional challenge."

Luntz is also credited with reframing "offshore drilling" to the more positive and optimistic "energy exploration," something fossil fuel companies use as often as they can to this day.[5] Even the term "environmentalist," he warned, has the "connotation of extremism." It's better to use "conservationist" as that conveys a "moderate, reasoned, common sense position."[6]

To be fair, in the years since, Luntz has publicly denounced his contributions to what clearly muddied the waters for many people. He now acknowledges that climate change is real, wants the federal government to do more to address the issue, and believes the Republican Party today should take the issue more seriously. Luntz also testified in front of a Senate Democratic climate panel in 2019 and, as reported by Anthony Adragna in *Politico*:

> urged Democrats to "personalize, individualize and humanize" the impacts of climate change to make it more relatable to the average person. He advised them to "jettison" language like describing the problem as a crisis in favor of phrases that motivate people to action. "Focus on the consequences of inaction," he said. "The American people want to know the positive of this, not just the negative. Not just the fear, they want to know the benefit of focusing on it."[7]

This, finally, is where Luntz and I agree and why I think he matters in this conversation. In the world of hyperpartisanship and tribal loyalty, I appreciate Luntz's change of heart. His evolution is a useful example for many still entrenched in their partisan identities.

More importantly, any rules for effective language created by experts in their fields, no matter what side of the aisle they fall on, should be taken seriously by those in the climate movement looking to build more effective campaigns.

As for "climate change" versus "global warming" and "environmentalist" versus "conservationist," awareness of the issue has progressed at least enough over the last twenty years to where switching one for another is no longer needed—at least in speaking to audiences who already care. But remember, Luntz's early advice on climate messaging was for a more skeptical audience—based on real sentiments he heard across the country from his conservative focus groups. In many places, these terms remain toxic today.

In 2017, I was in grad school running a student organization dedicated to clean energy and environmental policy solutions. I was headed to the UN climate conference that year and wanted to create a social media campaign to raise awareness about the importance of the negotiations with the general public. Too many around me seemed checked out. I decided to ask people the simple question: "What does climate change mean to you?" and film their short, unscripted responses for social media videos.

Whether or not I was subconsciously tapping into Frank Luntz's and Tony Schwarz's best practices, I felt something was missing in how people thought about climate change. I wanted to tell stories that put a face to an issue so many people feel is still so abstract or far away in the future. I wanted to create a question that forced people to think about the issue from a personal and direct perspective—to see themselves, their lives, their families, and their futures in their answers.

These were just some of the responses we received from dozens of people across the country and even some from outside the United States: "I think catastrophic weather effects will affect the poor and deepen the refugee crisis," "I was a senior in high school when Hurricane Katrina struck and I went with a group of students to help families rebuild—to me climate change means action," "I'm from Hampton Roads, Virginia and my community, like so many coastal communities, are threatened," "I don't think my Baby-Boomer generation has given enough credence to climate science because perhaps it won't affect us that much but I'm happy my children's and grandchildren's generations are stepping up to address the problem," "I'm surrounded by people who don't think climate change is real, but I think we are seeing constant extremes and natural disasters and it's clear that this is something we need to take action on," "I'm from Florida, and climate change to me means a lot of uncertainty and not knowing what kinds of challenges and risks me and my future children may face some day."

My student group and I didn't have the resources to launch our #ClimateChangeMeans social-media campaign to a very wide audience. But the limited success we achieved stuck with me as an effective way to get people to think about climate change from a personal perspective. There were even some climate skeptics in my family who surprised me by submitting videos, speaking from a place of genuine reflection. The question was so simple and open-ended that it allowed for people to participate in the message without being clouded by their ideologies. And I stressed there were no wrong answers. Climate change means something different to each of us, and that's okay. In fact, that's the point. But by asking the question, "What does climate change mean to *you*?" the issue was presented in a new way that made it possible for anyone to form a connection. This type of engagement is how we can increase issue identification. We must reframe how we think about climate change to make it personal, direct, and immediate.

Are You Better off Today Than You Were Four Years Ago?

Let's conduct another thought experiment to help reframe how we think about the issue of climate change. One of the most potent political campaign questions of all time was the question Ronald Reagan posed to then-President Jimmy Carter during their 1980 presidential debate, "Are you better off today than you were four years ago?"

Reagan tapped into resentments many voters shared about the job Carter had done as president—rightly or wrongly. It was a very simple frame that covered any negative feeling voters might have felt toward foreign policy, the economy, the general state of things, or anything else happening in their lives. This question has been used effectively many times since, including by Donald Trump's campaign in 2024 when it took on new significance by tapping into voters' resentments over Covid restrictions, inflation, cost of living, immigration, and more. This is also another perfect example of Luntz's Ask-a-Question rule of effective language and Schwarz's Responsive Cord.

So let's borrow it. Let's ask everyone, "Are you better off today than you were four years ago?"—*specifically* in relation to the impacts we have seen from climate change during that time period. Alongside "What does climate change mean to you," this question invites people to reflect on real, tangible changes in their lives—and to consider how much has shifted in a short time. Were there as many catastrophic fires, oppressive heat waves, devastating floods, and pesky allergies just four years ago?

The four-year framing also aligns with presidential elections—which is, of course, how Reagan and others have used it to differentiate themselves from the actions of their predecessors. Similarly, voters who are asked this question can attribute their answers—and the increased climate impacts they've experienced—to whichever presidential administration was in power during that time period as an accountability tool. Was the president at this time taking action on climate change or rolling back environmental regulations? Did they respond well to the needs from natural disasters? Did they make me feel safer?

* * *

Movements that build grassroots and community connections by creating a narrative shift and reframing how their target audience thinks about the cause win, as Leslie Crutchfield showed. If all

American voters saw themselves in the issue of climate change, we would solve the problem of issue identification and be on our way to passing all the important policies, economic measures, and societal actions we need. The campaign case studies, ideas, and best practices of communication presented in this chapter can help us get there.

Issue identification is also strengthened the more we emotionally connect with our positive vision for the future and reimagine what a climate-resilient and sustainable society looks like. This can also reframe how we *think* about the issue as we build a compelling narrative around a decarbonized world.

To illustrate what I mean, let's dive into a few more ideas within our vision. It's important to keep coming back to this, even as we discuss more practical, in-the-moment campaign tactics. We must never lose sight of what we're working toward.

One Trillion Trees

When European settlers first arrived in the early 1600s, forests covered roughly half of what would become the landmass of the United States. Since then, total US forestland has seen a net reduction of approximately 257 million acres. That is more than three times the size of the total acreage under management by the National Park Service. It also equates to a great deal of stored carbon released back into the atmosphere.

Trees and grass take in carbon dioxide through their leaves and stalks, making them one of the best natural tools for carbon mitigation. This makes them a "carbon sink" as opposed to a "carbon source," like the burning of fossil fuels. It is estimated that US forests, grasslands, and other natural sources sequester around 850 million metric tons of CO_2 per year, which mitigates around 16 percent of total US CO_2 emissions. This is the equivalent of taking around fifty million cars off the road.[8]

Increasing the carbon sink in the near term may be our best hope to offset the emissions we can't reduce. This may buy us the time we need to fundamentally reshape society's relationship with energy production and consumption and avoid climate disaster. However, for plants to serve a more significant role in carbon sequestration, their total acreage needs to increase—a lot.

Under the Obama Administration, the United States developed the Mid-Century Strategy for deep decarbonization (MCS), which provides a vision for nationwide emissions reduction of 80–100 percent below 2005 levels by the year 2050. This was also required by Article 4, Paragraph 19 of the Paris Agreement that called on all countries to "formulate and communicate long-term low greenhouse gas emission development strategies."[9]

The MCS divides policy priorities into three categories: (1) transforming to a low-carbon energy system; (2) sequestering carbon through forests, soils, and CO_2 removal technologies; and (3) reducing non-CO_2 emissions. For each of these categories, well-researched policy plans are detailed with projection scenarios showing multiple pathways through which these policies might help achieve the MCS's long-term goal. One goal calls for expanding US forests and long-lived perennial grasses by 40–50 million acres. The MCS estimates this could potentially offset up to 50 percent of US emissions by mid-century.

This isn't just a Democratic idea. In 2020, President Trump signed an Executive Order to join the World Economic Forum's Trillion Trees Initiative, pledging to "plant, grow, conserve, and restore trees on American soil and around the world."[10] Climate change wasn't mentioned as a motivating factor—rather, the environmental and economic benefits of healthy and resilient forests and grasslands were highlighted. But many of the actions needed to meet this goal would be similar to Obama's mid-century strategy.

Companies, nonprofits, and governments have promoted planting campaigns for decades. Since the 1990s, the number of tree-planting groups working in the tropics, for instance, has increased by nearly 300 percent—with most of that increase occurring just within the last decade.[11] However, there are questions about the effectiveness of these efforts—from how well they're reaching target areas to the actual survival rates of planted trees to the long-term net impact in a world where deforestation is still widespread.

Still, in the United States, federal land management agencies theoretically have the tools needed to get the job done. The US Forest Service directly manages 193 million acres and "supports sustainable management" on 500 million more acres of private, state, and tribal forests. The Bureau of Land Management manages another 250 million acres, and the National Park Service manages 84 million acres. Of course, not all of this acreage is suitable for forest or grassland. But from 1987 to 2012, tree planting efforts helped US forests expand by roughly one million acres per year—with federal land agencies accounting for roughly a third of that.[12] To reach the mid-century reforestation goal, this annual expansion rate needs to double on average. And, since it takes time for trees to grow and reach their full carbon sequestration potential, higher rates of planting must occur in the near term. Projections call for 2.7 million acres per year of forest expansion from now through at least 2035.[13]

In 2022, President Biden's Bipartisan Infrastructure Law provided over $100 million to the US Forest Service for reforestation efforts. This will help plant more than a billion trees on national forest lands over the next decade—a much-needed investment.[14] But most of it will likely go to restoring forests that are being lost from wildfires, insects, diseases, hurricanes, tornadoes, and other climate hazards. In just 2020 and 2021, over 2.5 million acres of Forest Service lands burned. In 2019, 5.4 million acres were damaged by disease and insect pests.[15]

A rapid expansion of reforestation efforts to not only sustain existing forests against climate threats but also expand them into a much larger carbon sink will be difficult. There are also numerous policy implications from competing land use priorities. US forestland produces a variety of goods and services essential to the economy. Residential development and agriculture—two of the biggest drivers of forest loss—are necessary for population growth and food. A significant portion of US energy production, including 40 percent of coal production, comes from federally managed lands.[16]

While the challenges are significant, so too are the potential rewards. On private lands, planting more trees in urban locations, constructing more large buildings sustainably out of wood, and climate-smart agricultural partnerships could usher in new economic opportunities. The MCS contains a case study for this in Iowa, where an estimated 27 percent of cropland—seven million acres—may not be profitable in commodity crop production but could be well-suited to perennial grasses or agroforestry. This could help increase rural landowner incomes while improving soil health, reducing nutrient runoff, and providing other environmental co-benefits.

The Iowa example is one of many public-private partnerships that will be required to ensure climate change-related land use changes do not lead to lost economic profitability. Any plan to increase forests and grasslands will need to carefully balance wood and food production, living space, and energy needs over the next few decades.

Fortunately, the MCS estimates that up to fifty million acres of trees could be planted on agricultural land alone without compromising production. Through precision agriculture and agroforestry, the MCS makes many recommendations regarding enhancing agriculture to support large-scale carbon sequestration. This will, as the MCS describes, "improve soil quality, water and nutrient retention, and crop yields, all with minimal competition for land use."[17]

* * *

A related idea that further illustrates the importance of managing lands to enhance natural carbon sinks is biomass energy. An estimated thirty-one million acres of US farmland could be used to grow energy crops.[18] According to the Biomass Energy Resource Center (BERC) in Burlington, Vermont, perennial grasses were used on the prairie for heating before the Industrial Revolution and in places with little forest land. These grasses came to be known as "prairie coal." They are easy to grow, resilient, and sequester a great deal of carbon in their roots and soil. BERC states that "switchgrass used for heating has an energy output to input ratio of at least 10 to 1, compared to other bioenergy sources with output to input ratios around 1 to 1."[19]

It's also been reported that herbaceous grasses, another fast-growing perennial, planted on one acre of farmland are capable of producing an "average annual yield of herbaceous biomass sufficient to meet the annual space-and water-heating needs of an average home."[20]

With any biomass energy source, the stored carbon is released when burned for energy and will need to be capped and stored. This process is known as bioenergy with carbon capture and storage (BECCS). According to a July 2017 paper in *Energy Procedia*, if implemented on a large scale, models project BECCS could remove up to 616 gigatons of cumulative global CO_2 from the atmosphere by 2100.[21] This would be hugely consequential in combating warming as current annual global CO_2 emissions are around 37 gigatons.

Under the Biden Administration, the US Department of Agriculture explored potential BECCS applications under their "Building Blocks for Climate Smart Agriculture and Forestry." But there is a lot more research that needs to be done to understand the effectiveness of these ideas, their cost, and what potential ecological harm they could have on existing natural systems at such a large scale.

Still, we must take BECCS seriously. In over one hundred of the 116 scenarios presented by the Intergovernmental Panel on Climate Change for how we limit warming to 2°C by 2100, some form of BECCS, reforestation, or afforestation was included.[22]

* * *

During President Biden's term, an update to the MCS was submitted that goes even further than the Obama plan. In what is now known as the "Long-Term Strategy of the United States: Pathways to Net-Zero Greenhouse Gas Emissions by 2050," up to 133 million acres in the United States are identified as potentially suitable for reforestation efforts.[23]

So far in President Trump's second term, he has taken many steps that seem incompatible with his previous trillion trees order. In March 2025, he signed an Executive Order to "Rapidly Expand Timber Production" on federal lands.[24] Still, the US long-term decarbonization strategy remains a valuable assessment—one our country will need to eventually return to in order to achieve our goals. It is also an official document that has been submitted to the United Nations Framework Convention on Climate Change, which means it will be easy for future administrations to pick up again.

* * *

All this talk of mid-century might seem a long way off, especially in the context of policy making. However, from a global climate standpoint, the importance of urgent action over the next few years cannot be overstated. The public and private sectors can work together to innovate in electric vehicles, "green" buildings, and energy—all of which will drive down emissions. But we are still unlikely to achieve net-zero by mid-century without massively bolstering our carbon sink.

These "nature-based solutions" also include coastal wetlands, salt marshes, and other "Blue Carbon" sources. Blue Carbon is stored in marine ecosystems, rich in biodiversity, that provide resilience against storms and floods to nature and people alike. These ecosystems sequester around 3 billion metric tons of carbon dioxide equivalent in their soils—which make them a very important part of any conversation about carbon sinks.[25] But they are some of the most threatened ecosystems on Earth. More global awareness and conservation efforts are needed just to keep much of our existing Blue Carbon intact.

Thankfully, the potential for increasing nature-based solutions on land to help achieve global climate goals is high. All told, around 28 percent of the entire US land mass is federally managed lands.[26] An even greater amount is held by privately owned farms.[27] The key to success will be accountability, which can only be achieved through robust measurement, reporting, and verification of results over time. Coordinated efforts between federal and state agencies, as well as private and tribal landowners, will be needed.

Reaching reforestation goals of 40–50 million acres would also recover roughly one-third of all US forestland lost since 1850. Imagine how that would transform many urban and rural areas alike to provide greater habitat and biodiversity for native species, better air and water quality, more recreational opportunities, and greater integration of humanity within the natural world. This is another example of a climate solution with mitigation and adaptation dual benefits that builds resilience to the changing world.

* * *

It doesn't take much to reframe how we think about the issue of climate change. Not when we see what it means to us in a more direct and personal way. And especially once we start imagining all the amazing things that will transform our lives for the better along the road to net zero.

But how we talk about it matters.

In the next chapter, we'll explore words that work when talking to different audiences about the causes and consequences of climate change, as well as some words that are clearly not effective. We'll also take a closer look at the images and narratives that have come to define the climate movement and how these messages may be helping—or hurting—our message.

Todd Stern, who led President Obama's climate policy team at the State Department in the years leading up to the passage of the Paris Agreement, delivered a speech on the future of the agreement a few years after it was passed. In the speech, he stated, "we can accomplish what we need to—if we have the political will."[28]

Here's how we build that political will.

7

Reframing How We Talk about Climate Change

Take a moment to think about an image related to climate change—what comes to mind? A polar bear? A melting glacier?

What I always see is the iconic image of a human hand holding the entire Earth in its palm—one side of the planet Garden of Eden, the other fire and brimstone. You've probably seen some version of it. The message is clear: there are two paths ahead—one of sustainability, one of destruction. I mostly agree with the overall frame, simplistic as it is. But by choosing these specific visuals, the activist image conveys a message about the power of humanity to "save the Earth." There's nothing specific about the threats we face. It's a powerful image for those who already care about climate change, not for those who don't.

Images are powerful. They're the language of movements. But for years, climate communications have relied on the same stale visuals. We can all understand how water melts from a glacier and pours endlessly into an ocean that is bound to rise. We see versions of Hell from the terror of world-on-fire imagery. We despair seeing a starving polar bear on a dwindling piece of sea ice. Well, at least some of us do. It is easy to fall back on these popular images in our communications. But beneath them is a deeper, unspoken message: that human civilization and nature are locked in opposition—when one rises, the other falls.

This binary framing fails to expand the climate conversation. It traps us in a false choice: save nature or save humanity. I intend to shake us out of this mental trap.

* * *

What if I told you that the Earth doesn't care about you?

That's the message I delivered in a 2022 TEDx talk I gave about the importance of reframing our climate conversations in order to overcome polarization. It sounds harsh—but it's true. Nature doesn't love or hate us. It simply is. Hurricanes don't care who's in their path. Wildfires don't choose their victims.

As a message, it is intended as a departure from the nature-savior messages of old. It reframes how we think about the "climate crisis" as a "humanity crisis." We're not trying to save the planet—we're trying to save ourselves! The planet doesn't need saving. We do.

I learned how much the Earth didn't care about me after Hurricane Katrina and in Alaska. It's been reinforced many times since. Let's make sure our climate images and messages reflect a sobering and realistic view of how much we are at risk. By recognizing our shared vulnerability, we can build shared purpose. We can do this in a way that doesn't further unhelpful climate doomism as we work toward a positive vision of the future we design to save us. This empowers us as the agents of change. It can bind us together in a shared sense of purpose to defeat our common enemy—rising temperatures.

As Dr. Hannah Ritchie writes in a section of her book, *It's Not the End of the World: How We Can Be the First Generation to Build a Sustainable Planet*, ". . . I've found that trying to build an environmental worldview based on the latest wildfire or hurricane is no good." She goes on to say, "if we take several steps back, we can see something truly radical, game-changing, and life-giving: humanity is in a truly unique position to build a sustainable world." She concludes, "doomsday attitudes are often no better than denial . . . accepting defeat on climate change is an indefensibly selfish position to take."[1]

Meet People Where They Are

In 2012, I was campaign manager on a race for the US House of Representatives in Ohio. A battleground district in a battleground state during a presidential election year. Unfortunately, we lost, but I worked with an amazing team and learned a lot about campaigns and elections. My boss, an unapologetic pro-choice female small-business owner, would have made an excellent member of Congress and would have supported many important issues I cared about. That's what elections are—the opportunity to make a difference on the big issues. But, as James Carville says, "to bring about change or to have a more just society, far and away the best way to accomplish that is through political power. Without political power, you're not going to get your shit done."[2]

The three obstacles presented in Chapter 3—a polarized electorate, paralysis by those who care (aka: the need to empower more people to engage in the process), and stale/ineffective messaging toward the audiences you need to reach—are faced by all candidate campaigns and issue campaigns alike. I faced them in the Ohio race and others. Effective campaigns are built around overcoming these fundamental challenges.

Our media consultant in Ohio was Ben Nuckels. Ben remains a friend and has continued to run and win many successful campaigns over the last decade. He was the media strategist for Wisconsin Governor Tony Evers' victory over Governor Scott Walker, which the Washington Post labeled, "... potentially the greatest Democratic victory of the [2018] midterms."[3] In the final week of the 2025 Wisconsin Supreme Court race between liberal candidate Susan Crawford and conservative Brad Schimel, Ben's firm was tasked with creating an ad to cut through the noise in what had become the most expensive judicial race in American history. His now-famous "Knee Pad Brad" ad—using audio of Schimel bragging about needing knee pads to beg for billionaire donations—helped push Crawford to victory. The ad highlighted the corruption of big spending by outside groups, which resonated with many voters on election day.

Ben has worked for many members of Congress, state and local candidates, labor organizations, and private companies. He listens to focus groups all over the country, speaking to voters on numerous issues. Ben knows how to move people. He's a messaging expert. When I asked what makes a campaign succeed, he said:

> for many campaigns, there's the mindset of—are we a persuasion or mobilization campaign? But often what I've found in the battleground states is that it's not an either/or proposition, it's an and/both. You have to persuade but also people don't *want* to be

persuaded. "I'm not persuaded by political ads," they might tell you in a focus group. So you have to provide them with the stimuli to come to their own conclusions. It's about the guttural stuff, the stuff that means something to them in their daily lives. Our job as campaign practitioners is to move people. To motivate them, to persuade them. We test a bunch of messages, we find what works. Campaign strategy is really about two questions: what do you want to say and who do you want to say it to? Then you can answer the question of *how* do you say it—that's the tactical piece, the mobilization piece.

Ben put this strategy to effective use in the Tony Evers for Governor campaign. One of the things they did was create county-level advertising in most of the seventy-two counties in Wisconsin, even in ones that had just ten or twenty thousand residents. Over 2.6 million votes were cast in the election, but Evers won with just 29,000 more votes than his opponent. Investment in county-level advertising that targeted very localized messages to what people cared about in those counties—small business investment, how many miles of roads or bridges were built—paid off. In other larger and more diverse counties where it made sense, the campaign talked about how many miles you'd have to drive to get to the nearest clinic for reproductive care and how their opponent was an anti-abortion extremist—setting up a clear difference in choice between the two candidates in the race.

If there's one phrase that sums up these tactics, it is this: meet people where they are. City dwellers, suburban commuters, rural voters—they care about different things. And they respond to different messages. One campaign in one state may need seventy-two different county-level messages. A national movement needs a mosaic of messages. But is the climate movement meeting people where they are? Maybe some, but everyone?

First Rule of Climate Change, Don't Talk about Climate Change

In the early weeks of Donald Trump's second term, shock and outrage emerged as government websites scrubbed the words "climate change" from official pages and documents. This happened in his first term as well. Of course, these changes came alongside Trump's burning desire to destroy any progress we'd made on fighting climate change and to increase fossil fuel extraction. But just the act of removing the words "climate change" from government websites did not mean much on its own.

In Florida, something similar occurred in early 2024. Republican Governor Ron DeSantis signed a bill that removed the words climate change from state statutes and deprioritized it from state policymaking decisions. Critics dubbed it the "Don't Say Climate Change" law.[4]

I get the anger over this; I share it. But here's the thing: we already know the phrase "climate change" is polarizing. In some communities, it shuts down conversations before they start. I would like to grant permission to people working on the front lines of this issue to *not* talk about climate change.

The *First Rule of Climate Change, Don't Talk about Climate Change* is a messaging concept borrowed from the 1999 movie *Fight Club*. This isn't to be taken literally in every situation. But there are many instances when injecting the words "climate change" into the conversation can be detrimental. As the Pew poll highlighted in Chapter 2 shows, partisan affiliation determines perceptions and beliefs about climate change more strongly than the local conditions actually experienced. Framing a poll, campaign, or conversation from the perspective of climate change may kick people into their corners. Is the goal to be right—or to be effective?

Language matters. We can talk about building resilience to floods and storms, to the impacts people are feeling in their communities, to the need for cleaner air—we can meet people where they are and listen to what they care about. We can do all this without being puritanical about including "climate change" in every conversation we have. At least not at first. We do need to connect to the issue eventually, or at least to specific policy proposals. But we can start at different places for different audiences.

This approach fits with Ben's framing of persuasion alongside mobilization. We have to mobilize the base of people who already care about this issue with the images and messages that work for them. We also have to persuade new audiences with more specific things they care about, appealing to them on a more universal communications platform. This is what the "Life" and "Love" campaigns did.

When Ben sits in focus groups, he is always looking for what he calls the "exit ramps"—the ways people emotionally disengage from messages they don't like. He might test a message that says, "candidate X improved the local economy by $10 million," but a respondent might say, "yeah, but what about *my* paycheck?" Or he might test a message about climate change but get a response from someone who says, "the world hasn't ended yet!" Those responses are exit ramps that prevent those people from absorbing the message.

To break through, you have to establish the fact pattern of what voters care about and don't care about. You test a bunch of issues and you get 16 percent support here or 40 percent there. But then you ask questions that get voters to open up about what's bothering them. You find the areas of agreement and you reframe your message to align with theirs. You localize. You personalize. You meet people where they are.

The Right Messengers

With better localized messages that connect to people's specific interests, we can move into the "how" of communication—the mobilization piece. And in this phase, the messenger matters just as much as the message.

Find the right validators that folks will listen to in the places they live. They need to be authentic. An environmentalist talking about climate change will simply be tuned out in many red states.

I've experienced the importance of finding the right messengers on every campaign I've ever worked on—regardless of the issue. But its relevance to climate change was driven home for me in conversation with Alex Posner, a Gen Zer who's made a national name for himself through his "EcoRight" conservative climate activism and advocacy. When Alex was in college just a few years ago, the fossil fuel divestment movement was dominant on his campus. Student activists urged their school to remove investments from fossil fuels (through their endowment and other investments). These efforts have gained popularity on college campuses around the country and, in recent years, have been one of the main ways for a young person concerned about climate change to plug into action. But, as Alex explained, there wasn't a broad set of tactics and messages that felt authentic to everyone nor aligned with everyone's values.

Alex told me that many young conservatives deeply care about the environment, climate change, and want to engage, but don't feel included by the messages of the climate left. He criticized how the current movement often elevates scolding voices, links itself to overly progressive social issues, and leans heavily into anti-capitalist rhetoric. It's fine for progressive voices to find their place in climate activism, of course. But the problem is when the movement *only* elevates these voices at the expense of engaging a broader range of perspectives. Doing so can warp public perception and contribute to a misbranding of climate change as an exclusively "Liberal" issue.

Alex also talked about how many climate messages promote the language of scarcity over the language of abundance. There's too much emphasis on what we have to limit or give up. For example, not traveling on planes, giving up meat, or any of the carbon footprint-oriented messages. Alex and his conservative peers want more optimistic and abundance-oriented messages that invite audiences into an optimistic vision of the future.

All of this led Alex to create a new organization, "Students for Carbon Dividends," which came together with a chorus of other conservative student groups to endorse a national climate plan—the first time something like that had really happened, he explained.

I agree with Alex on many points. I was also surprised to hear how young conservatives feel there isn't a place for them in the national conversation about an issue they care about, simply because they come at it from a different perspective. It raises a hard question: is the climate movement fundamentally structured to work across the aisle? It may seem unfair to blame the well-intentioned climate activist after so many years of obstruction, mostly coming from one political party. But if our messages are alienating potential allies, that's a strategic failure we must address.

Building bipartisan support is not a luxury, it's a necessity. Around 85 percent of congressional seats are in "safe" districts where incumbents face very little challenge from the other side. This means the battle for control over Congress is over only about 15 percent of seats. Going into the 2026 midterms, for example, the Cook Political Report rates only forty of the 435 House seats up for re-election as having competitive races—9 percent.[5] Of the thirty-five Senate seats up in 2026, which includes the special elections in Florida and Ohio, only six are rated as competitive—a slightly better 17 percent.[6] You can wait until your team is in power and try to jam through as much progress as you can on the issues you care about in the two to four years before control flips back to the other side and likely reverses everything. Or, you can take the steps needed to build longer-term and more meaningful bipartisan strategies. And since most seats are safe, most election outcomes are now determined in primaries. If you're committed to building bipartisanship, this means engaging in Republican primaries. Alex pointed out that the environmental movement is missing in action in Republican primaries. That will have to change.

If you decide this is all too hard and wait for your team to be in power again, you may be waiting a long time. Since the Second World War, after one political party loses full control of government—that is control over the House, Senate, and presidency—they've had to wait, on average, fourteen years to regain unified government again.[7] Past results don't predict future outcomes. Still, we can't operate under the mindset that "we're just one election cycle away" from unified Democratic control and all the climate policies we've long dreamed of. We don't have time for that. It is bipartisanship or bust.

Coming from very different perspectives, the heart of what both Alex and Ben are saying is that many campaigns and movements get stuck on the message they want to convey and not on the audiences who will receive it. Protests, sit-ins, and other ways to engage in primaries on both sides of the aisle can force advocates to create unique messages. If done effectively—through constructive engagement on policy themes that resonate with those audiences—Democratic and Republican candidates alike can be turned into authentic messengers on environmental and climate solutions, even if neither of those words is used. We can reframe how we talk to focus on disaster and resilience planning, abundance and economic growth, immediate and human needs.

Primaries are often hyperlocal. That's a strength. You can push candidates to outline detailed plans: How will you protect this community from flooding; from wildfire or extreme temperatures? How will you clean up local pollution? How will you create jobs with solar or wind infrastructure?

Unfortunately, we're never going to have the resources to run a nationwide climate campaign that targets different messages to our more than 3,000 counties or that knocks on every door in 435 congressional districts. But we can tailor what works for different audiences and find the right messengers who can speak to their values and priorities. We need to keep our national champions who already care about the issue, and how we talk to them may look the same as it always has. But we also need new champions who may need a completely different approach.

Newton's Third Law of Politics

I want to commend Alex and young conservatives like him for approaching the issues of climate change and emissions reductions from a genuine place of concern. There is a lot of pressure in the modern conservative movement to conform to the politics of Donald Trump and to those who deny climate change is real, question the human impact, and advocate for fossil fuels at all costs. Young people on college campuses today are caught in the middle of culture-war politics that push and pull them in different ideological directions with whiplash speed. This contest for young hearts and minds breaks down along many of the same polarized and partisan lines as our national politics. For over a decade, no one led the charge more than Charlie Kirk.

In 2012, at just 18 years old, Charlie Kirk started his organization, Turning Point USA, with the help of Tea Party activist Bill Montgomery. Fourteen years later, Turning Point USA has chapters on over 3,500 high school and college campuses, over 250,000 student members, and hundreds of staff. The organization describes itself as "the largest and fastest growing conservative youth activist organization in the country."[8]

Kirk spread conservative principles of free market, limited government, American exceptionalism, and more among his chapters. Along with his political action organization—Turning Point Action—Kirk and Turning Point USA used their power and reach to register students to vote, bring conservative speakers to campuses, empower young people to engage in elections at all levels to support conservative candidates, and, most importantly, to support President Trump's agenda. Kirk was one of President Trump's closest allies, and he joked on California Governor Gavin Newsom's podcast in March of 2025 that he spoke with Trump "once or twice a week." Kirk's social media reached over 100 million people per month, he had one of the most engaged Twitter handles in the world and was host of the popular podcast "The Charlie Kirk Show." Tens of millions of dollars flowed into Turning Point USA, Turning Point Action, and other Kirk ventures each year.

I don't know what Kirk's stance was on every issue. But, on the issue of climate change, I watched a video he posted on YouTube called "Charlie Kirk Crushes Know-It-All With 3 Simple Questions."[9] The video was viewed more than half a million times in the first few months it was uploaded. In it, Kirk is at the mic engaged in one of his trademark "ask me anything" debate styles at UC Santa Barbara. A student asks him a series of questions about the increased climate impacts we're seeing, transitioning away from fossil fuels, and climate science. His cellphone in his hand for quick reference, the student pulls up reports and studies to back up his claims. The student gets no concessions from Kirk but, instead, faces a barrage of questions thrown back at him in Kirk's "Whataboutism" debate style.

I think the student does an excellent job holding his own against Kirk and against what looks like an audience of hundreds of pro-Kirk hecklers who start shouting at him when the back-and-forth gets tense. The student makes clear and reasoned points backed by data and facts in the face of Kirk's pro-fossil fuel skepticism that human activity plays any part in global warming. At one point, the student calls Kirk out for creating a straw man argument as Kirk switches to a belligerent line of questioning about the environmental harms around critical minerals mining and EV battery production/disposal (in response to the student's question about ending fossil fuel subsidies and investing in renewable energy sources)—completely separate issues.

But trying to win an argument against Kirk using data and "scientific consensus" is where the student makes his fundamental mistake. He's trying to win with science. But you can't fact-check someone out of a belief they didn't form with facts. And you can't win the room by appealing only to logic.

What if the student had taken a different approach? What if he had said, "you know, we can disagree on what's causing the temperature to rise but we do know it's rising"—a point Kirk acknowledges at the beginning of the video. "So shouldn't we invest in our twenty-first-century economy that can create many new innovative clean technologies that improve our standards of living and support hundreds of thousands of jobs?"

What if the student didn't mention climate change at all but instead talked about the human crises caused by extreme heat, floods, fires, and disasters that hit the places we live, and our need to build resilience that keeps us safe? What if he appealed to the heightened emotions and anxieties of the young people in the crowd in a less data-driven and more visceral way, as Kirk does, that made them think about the future they wish to build, inherit, and pass along to their kids? What if he provided a vision for a sustainable future that felt exciting, not punishing?

None of this would have been likely to change Kirk's mind. But perhaps it would have resonated with some in the audience—meeting them where they are in a more effective way. Kirk himself started as a lone voice, going into the "lion's den" of liberal college campuses to peel off moldable young minds one at a time. As climate advocates, we too should engage diverse audiences that don't always agree with us, using better language and ideas to overcome divides. There are messages that could resonate with at least some who are perhaps just being swept up because there aren't alternatives that they feel consider their points of view, and that's what they see their friends doing.

As our national politics swing back and forth in partisan polarization, a rule has developed that maps to Sir Isaac Newton's Third Law of Motion from the 1600s. This states that for every action, there is an equal and opposite reaction. Applied to politics, for every Greta Thunberg activist, you get a Charlie Kirk; for every Obama, you get a Trump; for every Anthony Fauci, you get an RFK Jr.; for every Bill Gates, you get an Elon Musk; for every New York Times Daily podcast, you get a Joe Rogan; and so on. Call this "Newton's Third Law of Politics."

It's not a new insight. But it matters, because it predicts backlash. If we understand that backlash is inevitable, we can stop being surprised when it comes. We can plan for it. Narrowly applied to the issue of climate change, it can give us a blueprint for cycles of progress and backlash we know will occur as we move toward solutions that inevitably disrupt entrenched special interests and industries. We can use this rule to stop getting forced into reactive strategies against counter movements of political resentment. We can't afford to stall out every four years after eking out minor climate victories. We need to train climate advocates and leaders who can adapt and intellectually spar with anyone holding any point of view in an "ask me anything" style.

All of this requires on-the-ground grassroots organizing across the country. The climate movement has had large and small grassroots movements for many years. But what Turning Point USA and other examples show us is that these new groups are tapping into a huge amount of grassroots energy and enthusiasm that is, in some cases, in direct opposition to climate progress. This is where a more inclusive and bipartisan climate movement can help. This is why radically reframing how we talk about climate change isn't a nice-to-have; it's a must. And why studying the best practices of successful campaigns and movements is time well spent—especially in how our current images, messages, and tactics may not be working to reach new and receptive audiences. Using Newton's Law of Politics, we can gain a better understanding of the popular culture drivers of our time and overcome roadblocks. When we put all these pieces together, we will be able to outmaneuver and outorganize anyone.

In September 2025, Kirk was tragically, and horrifically, shot and killed during a speaking engagement in front of a large crowd. We must be able to remain free to share our ideas, vigorously debate with one another, and engage in our institutions and democratic processes to make positive change without the threat of violence. Political violence must always be condemned.

Global Warming's Six Americas

We don't have to search through the wilderness very far to find better strategies for how we can talk about climate change with different audiences. We already have the data. And it turns out, the country doesn't split neatly into two camps—progressive or conservative—on this issue. Apparently, there are six distinct groups we must consider.

For over a decade, the Yale Program on Climate Change Communications has studied how the American public identifies with the issue of climate change. As they explain, "public engagement efforts must start with the fundamental recognition that people are different and have different psychological, cultural, and political reasons for acting—or not acting—to reduce greenhouse gas emissions."[10]

Their research has identified six unique audiences, each responding to the issue of climate change in different ways, ranging from those convinced it's happening and that immediate action needs to be taken, to those who don't really think about it, to those who strongly believe it's *not* happening. These are "Global Warming's Six Americas," as Yale has named their study, and they are the: Alarmed, Concerned, Cautious, Disengaged, Doubtful, and Dismissive.[11]

A hopeful finding: as of 2024, Dismissives make up only 10 percent of the population. As Dr. Katherine Hayoe explains in her book *Saving Us, A Climate Scientist's Case for Hope and Healing in a Divided World*, Dismissives "are the only ones it's nearly impossible to have a positive conversation with. . . . For a Dismissive, disagreeing with the science of climate change is one of their strongest frames. It's so integral to who they are that it renders them literally incapable of considering something that they think would threaten their identity."[12]

That's frustrating—especially when those people are family, coworkers, or elected officials. We've all been there, and we tend to waste time trying to convince these people who will never be convinced—at least not by us and not by what we may think are well-reasoned arguments supported by data and facts. But Hayoe goes on to explain that we *can* have constructive conversations and make a difference with each of the other five categories, which together represent 90 percent of the population.

These six climate audiences exist across Democrats and Republicans, across urban and rural America, and any of our other perceived divides. Specifically tailoring messages to better engage each one may help us solve some of these divides and find common ground.

For instance, the Alarmed and Concerned (54 percent of the population) take climate change seriously and support policies to address it. But Yale's research found many of them don't know what they personally can do to help. That's where we come in—with tools for action and empowerment.

Meanwhile, nearly all of the strategies discussed over the previous pages and chapters apply to how we can better appeal to and engage the Cautious and the Doubtful (30 percent of the population). Furthermore, the category of the Disengaged is one that deeply concerns me, and I've dedicated the beginning of the following chapter to it. Yale defines this category as just 5 percent of the population. But, certainly, this increases when taking low voter turnout and apathetic political engagement into consideration. Still, the bottom line is that the *Six Americas* study shows 90 percent of Americans are at least open to climate conversations. That's a massive opportunity.

Yale, Dr. Hayhoe, and others have done incredible work helping us quantify who is reachable on the issue of climate change and what messages they might be receptive to—if those messages are crafted with specific audiences in mind. The "how" of this work is murkier, which is where our campaign best practices come in. Taking these lessons to reframe how we think and talk about the issue will increase identification and make change with all audiences—including ourselves. We may also need a fresh approach to keep us motivated. Remember that the seventh rule of *Fight Club* is: "the fight will go on as long as it has to."

Urgency and Generational

In March of 2025, the Potential Energy Coalition partnered with the Yale Program on Climate Change Communications to publish a massive new study of 60,000 people across twenty-three countries. The goal of the study: Does the world want action on climate, and how can we motivate the public to accelerate progress?

Their report found many interesting and important message frames that can help build climate policy support in countries around the world, but two stood out. The first were messages that focused on the sense of urgency to protect ourselves from extreme weather, to protect our health, and other immediate impacts. The second were messages about protecting the next generation. According to their findings, "Across every country, love for the next generation was the dominant reason for action on climate change. This reason was 12 times more popular than creating jobs. . . . The data clearly showed that one message moves the whole world significantly: protecting the planet for the next generation."[13] This message had positive effects across the political spectrum.

The study provides yet another empirical data point that well-tailored messages to the right audiences can promote support for climate action in every country. There is no silver bullet. But we can use the messages we know work, reframe the ones we know don't, and build the base of support essential for policy action.

Still, we have to consider the real-world impacts on diverse populations and ensure our messages support policies that are carefully and equitably crafted for successful implementation. I spoke with a pollster who has implemented some of the "future gens" messaging suggestions and has seen it work with his clients. But he has also had clients go to Andhra Pradesh, in southern India, to try to run a campaign to increase regenerative farming practices by telling farmers it will be good for their children. Then, in focus groups, the farmers told him that if they adopt these practices, their yields will decrease and they aren't sure they will be in business next year, let alone the three to five years it takes to transition farmland to natural agricultural practices. Their current economic needs outweigh their future generations' needs. The prioritization of climate action against other needs can easily slip depending on the day-to-day issues at hand—just as voter turnout data showed it did in the 2024 US election.

As stated, many studies show massive majorities around the world support a wide array of climate actions. Future gens messaging and other frames can increase that support further. But support for action is not the bar we need to clear for action to happen. The public needs to demand action—it needs to be a high priority. That will happen when people understand how solving climate change can help solve their problems today. If we, as climate advocates, can't provide answers to today's problems, then that allows others to fill in those answers for us.

The next three chapters take everything we've learned about radically reframing how we think and talk about climate change and put it into practice to make real-world change. We'll cover the conversations we have, grassroots and community-level organizing, national policy engagement, and the personal and individual changes we may need to make within ourselves to build space for the rest of it.

8

How to Enact Change at the Personal Level

When I talked about the three major obstacles to solving climate change—polarization, paralysis, and stale, ineffective messaging—I made an assumption. That is, that people are actually *hearing* about the issue enough to become polarized or paralyzed. But what about voters who don't follow politics or are otherwise difficult to reach through traditional advocacy efforts? How do we reach them?

At the height of the 2024 presidential election, 69 percent of Americans said they were following news about the candidates very or fairly closely.[1] But, according to Gallup, after paying heightened attention during Presidential election years, people tend to disengage. The percentage of Americans who report they follow national political news "very closely" drops to between 30 and 40 percent in non-election years.[2] Since there are smaller but still very important elections in most places every year, the term "nonelection years" is misleading. But if you disengage from the political process, as most Americans do, until billions of campaign dollars during presidential years break through, you might not know much about the importance of these local elections or the important issues being decided by them—which could include climate policies.

To make matters worse, many people who don't follow politics actively *avoid* politics, political discussions, or anything with messaging that sounds, to them, "political." This may have happened to you, trying to engage friends or family members on the warming climate only to have them respond "oh, I don't like to talk about politics."

It's understandable, but frustrating. Caring about the planet shouldn't be political. But the polarization around climate change makes it hard to even start a conversation—which makes it harder to talk about solutions.

In a 2024 interview, *New York Times* opinion contributor Ezra Klein spoke with Yanna Krupnikov, who wrote the book *The Other Divide: Polarization and Disengagement in American Politics*. Krupnikov argues that the *biggest* divide in American politics is not between Democrats and Republicans, "Left" versus "Right," or urban versus rural. It is between those who follow politics closely and those who pay almost no attention to it.[3] If you are a Democrat who follows politics closely, for instance, you are likely to have more in common with a *Republican* who also follows politics closely than with someone of your own party who does not follow politics. At least you may see the world and understand the issues in similar ways. Those who don't follow politics, on the other hand, may list completely different issues as their top concerns. And yet, most importantly, many who don't follow politics still vote and still need to be reached.

Then there are those who are eligible to vote but don't or who vote infrequently. This latter group is known as low-propensity voters. In 2024, both the Harris and Trump campaigns heavily prioritized strategies to engage low-propensity voters as they usually fall into the "independent" category, which is so critical to outcomes in the swing states.[4] Novel media and outreach strategies were developed to bring these voters back into the fold. To give you a sense of how many people there are in these disengagement categories and how big an impact they can have, more than 85 million eligible voters did not vote in 2024. That is a far higher number than the total votes cast for either Trump or Harris. According to the Environmental Voter Project, "If 'Did Not Vote' had been a presidential candidate, they would have beaten Donald Trump by 9.1 million votes, and they would have won 21 states, earning 265 electoral college votes to Trump's 175 and Harris's 98. As in most US elections, the real swing voters in 2024 were those deciding between voting or not voting."[5]

The dual challenges of those who disengage from politics but still vote and those who disengage from voting either altogether or by voting infrequently in any given election, especially in smaller and local elections, present real problems. Disengagement has a tremendous impact on our elections and upends our strategies for how to reach the audiences we need. It also transcends polarization and traditional partisanship divides. How do you—as a candidate, party, or issue advocate—get through to people if they are, by definition avoiding you but may still influence the outcome of critical elections either by voting consistently on issues you may not agree with or by staying home and not voting on an issue you think they should be?

Another way to think about it is this: most modern-day US elections are not a choice between Candidate A and Candidate B, they are a choice between each of those candidates and the couch.

Disengagement is another obstacle to solving the issue of climate change, to be sure. But it wasn't included as such earlier because the key to addressing it leads to a much more personal discussion of individual motivation. Conservative journalist Andrew Breitbart coined a doctrine that "politics is downstream of culture," and that to change politics one must first change culture.[6] While I may not agree with Breitbart on much, and while his statement might not apply to every issue, I think it rings true in the issue of climate change. In many cases, I also think culture can be downstream from politics, and they can switch back and forth at different times as cultural awareness shifts our politics and vice versa. Building issue identification is once again the key to overcoming disengagement—the culture change that flows both up and downstream into our politics. But how do you change culture with the hard to reach?

Fundamental Human Truths

Kelly Ward Burton served as the Executive Director of the Democratic Congressional Campaign Committee—the committee that works to elect Democrats to the House of Representatives. She also ran the National Democratic Redistricting Committee—a joint project of President Barack Obama and former Attorney General Eric Holder—to fight for fair maps and push back against political gerrymandering.

Kelly is an incredible campaigner, motivator, and manager of people. She believes that there are fundamental human truths that underpin great campaigns and movements: People want to be heard, seen, and want to know you care about them, respect them, and are fighting for them. The best movements and campaigns use grounding tactics that speak to these basic human motivations. You can think of this as an extension of meeting people where they are. But Kelly takes it to an even deeper level we often don't consider until culture and politics have changed so quickly and dramatically that we have to stop and reassess what just happened.

There are many voters who believe Donald Trump saw, heard, respected, and fought for them. He was elected for it—twice. This might be missing from the analysis of someone who didn't vote for him and sees many of his actions as exactly the opposite, at least toward their values. But there are best practices here to consider both for candidate campaigns of the future that can rebuild our broken politics and for solving the issue of climate change.

We often think about campaigns or advocacy efforts as top-down, led by national organizations with large budgets or charismatic individuals. But Kelly sees the moment we're in now differently.

> We need to really *see* each other, rebuild the connective tissue between us, and restore the sense of community many of us feel we're missing, in real life and not online. By focusing on the fundamentals of our communities and strengthening our human connections, we'll rebuild trust with one another. And maybe that's how we'll remember that we're all connected—that what happens to one matters to all.

Kelly describes Trump's second term as an "earthquake," a "seismic shift." The world has changed; politics has fundamentally changed. What's worked in advocacy until now may not work any longer. We have to rebuild from the ground up, and that has to look different than it did before. Society can't go back to the way it was. I've heard these sentiments echoed by others who work in campaigns and advocacy right now. But even with all these changes, the fundamental truths of what people need and how to reach them remain the same, Kelly believes. That's the true heart of the grassroots.

To rebuild our grassroots movements and be ready for one-on-one work to reconnect with others, we may need to build personal space within ourselves. Kelly sees humility and practice as the key to this. In times when everything seems to be upended, we must remain humble and thoughtful about the questions we need to ask ourselves and one another to understand what's coming next and where we're going from here. Be skeptical of anyone who claims to have the "truth" or the "one right way" of what we should do. Even if you think you know the path forward, you still have to listen and check your own ego, not once but all the time. Find value in what others have to say, even if they disagree with you. This can make our climate conversations and all levels of our engagement much more effective because it's giving people what they ultimately need and want—to be seen, heard, and valued.

Inner Transformation

Kelly is mostly talking about solving our broken politics, but she believes this work has to happen within us as well. Among some in environmental and climate circles, there is also a growing belief that to solve global climate change we must first turn inward. They believe inner transformation is needed to reconnect ourselves to nature and reclaim something ethereal we may have "lost" along the way to forming our rapid, always-on, digital and impersonal modern society. Call this, once again, reconnecting with our fundamental human truths. Ideas like this have been around since the early days of the environmental "treehugger" movement; since the Buddha. As the practical and pragmatic person I am, I've resisted them. I have a deep and personal connection to nature. But what does that have anything to do with the policies we need to solve climate change?

I'm starting to think differently. In 2024, I joined the Mind Body Ecology Institute (MBEI) as an advisor to explore a new path in my understanding of climate solutions. Their online and in-person immersive nature-based programs, eco workshops, talks, and film screenings are dedicated to "exploring Earth care + self care practices to promote sustainable living and flourishing." MBEI seeks to counter the Western notion of the self as separate from nature, with dominion over it.[7]

In their message, there is a pragmatic and effective climate advocacy message. If we aren't separate from nature, then this work can help us see the value in solutions that safeguard both people and the planet for the long term. We flourish as part of nature.

This can also combat climate anxiety.

My journey to mindfulness, inner transformation, brain training—call it whatever you like—started in Alaska but fully budded on political campaigns where I pushed myself to my limits and experienced panic attacks from the long hours and intense level of stress. From then on, I have strived to hone a daily practice of mindfulness meditation. The RAIN technique helps train my brain to handle unwanted intrusive thoughts—Recognize, Accept, Investigate, Non-attachment. I've found this to be a powerful tool against the darkest of nights where the flood of trauma, anxiety, and stress can seem overwhelming. It has helped me recover from near-death experiences, the devastation of catastrophic storms, the stress of daily life, and the anticipatory anxiety of an uncertain future in a radically changed climate.

This is not to say developing your own mindfulness practice should make you feel any less urgent about our immediate climate needs. But too much anxiety can lead to paralysis or disengagement. Climate doomism is not helpful to any of the solutions we seek. We must build the space within us for empowerment. We must find coping strategies to keep ourselves motivated and engaged. It's ongoing work that will require us to hold two ideas in mind at once: we are small compared to the scale of the climate crisis, and we are still powerful enough to help shape its outcome.

101 Ways *You* Can Solve Climate Change

From the impacts we will experience to the inner transformations needed, the future of climate change is personal. That was the title of my 2022 TEDx talk, and I believe it even more strongly today. But there is no silver-bullet list of "101 things . . ." we can do in our daily lives that will solve climate change.

As Dr. Sweta Chakraborty, behavioral scientist and CEO of North America for the climate activist organization We Don't Have Time, said to me in a conversation we had about this:

Paying attention to our personal actions is critical to deep root universal values of environmental stewardship in us and in future generations. How we treat the planet must be taught worldwide—just as we teach our youth how to treat one another kindly. That said, the reality is that even a homeless person living in a fossil-fuel powered society has too high a carbon footprint. As long as oil, gas, and coal are fueling societal infrastructure, no one is sustainable. To suggest otherwise is nefarious propaganda by BP and other oil companies suggesting that we can impact our warming planet by consuming better or less. This strategy of shifting blame to the consumer whilst maintaining business as usual has allowed for the dirty energy sector to ensure that nothing changes.

So, to recap—we can enact personal change using reflection to build empowerment within ourselves and to overcome anxiety, apathy, and paralysis. We can branch out to others with humbleness, ready to listen, and with better tools of communication, empathy, and understanding—which can help us break through to those who might not be hearing about the issues we care about and are unreachable by traditional campaign tactics. We can reframe how we think and talk about climate change to increase issue identification both for us and in conversations with others. Enacting personal change in these ways can rebuild the connective tissue with others. It can help restore our sense of community and place. Cultural change starts with each of our individual actions and flows downstream into our movements and politics.

The next two chapters are about enacting change at larger scales. But change at every level depends on individual action. One of the most important actions you can take is to vote. But you won't vote if you don't think your voice matters or if you don't view policy decisions as part of the solution. You won't vote if you feel your community has been abandoned or betrayed by a lack of governmental action.

We must be properly motivated, and maybe that starts from within.

Run for Something

I know this is a stretch for most of us. We just got done talking about how disengaged so many of us are. Even for the most engaged, running for office can seem both personally impossible to fit into our busy lives and deeply unwelcome—why in the world would I want to *do* that to myself? We all hate politicians, why would I want to *become* one? And yet, as a person who has worked with many first-time candidates, I would be remiss not to at least try to plug this potential avenue.

We sometimes forget that elected office is about public service. We value the service of those in our military, of first responders, teachers, postal workers, and trash collectors. But because of the toxic nature of our polarized politics, the contributions of our elected officials often get lost. Many of the personalities of those we elect also don't help with our impressions of the offices they hold. They lie, manipulate, cheat, get bribed, get caught up in sex scandals, and sacrifice their integrity to cling to power. Even for those who don't, they may perpetuate a status quo that makes us feel unrepresented and unheard. But it doesn't need to be that way.

We can be the ones who step up and fight for change in the halls of Congress, in the state house, or in local government. I promise you, worse and less qualified people than you are running for important positions all over the country right now—many in uncontested local races because no one else is willing to step up and throw their hat into the ring. Even if you lose, facing any race at all could mean forcing your existing officials to take the issues you care about more seriously. If no one challenges them, why would they ever change?

Nancy Pelosi was a full-time mom raising five kids before she ever thought about running for office. She entered politics as a volunteer with her local party and over time became chair of her state party. She was first elected to Congress when she was forty-seven. She has now served nearly twenty terms and was the first woman elected Speaker of the House of Representatives.

Regardless of your politics, that path should inspire anyone. We all have to start somewhere. Often it is the experiences we have raising a family, running a business, serving in the military, or serving others in our community that make us the best candidates.

Be the change you wish to see. Start small. Run for something locally. There are many groups that offer resources for first-time candidates. You'll find your way.

9

How to Enact Change at the Local and Community Level

We often think of governmental action as something that only happens in Congress or the White House. And when a key federal policy fails, we assume it undermines our entire effort—right? In reality, the work to reduce the majority of our greenhouse gases as well as adaptive actions that strengthen disaster planning and build resilience in the places we live will happen *mostly* through state and local policymaking.

Cities account for more than 70 percent of global carbon pollution and consume most of the world's energy supply.[1] Yet, according to a 2020 Brookings report, fewer than half of the one hundred largest US cities have greenhouse gas emissions reduction targets.[2] A 2022 analysis by the American Council for an Energy-Efficient Economy found that of the thirty-eight largest US cities, twenty were on track to achieve mid-century Paris Agreement decarbonization targets—a slightly better 53 percent. However, the study noted, dozens of other large US cities do not have the necessary emissions data to effectively evaluate progress.[3]

Cities are far from being resilient systems capable of withstanding today's climate impacts. As the Intergovernmental Panel on Climate Change identified in their 2022 report on human vulnerability, cities, and settlements—and recent disasters have confirmed—current adaptation is unable to resolve the risk to urban areas in all world regions and for all hazard types. So, cities are both on the front lines of experiencing climate damages while also contributing a huge amount to the problem. Of course, not everyone lives in a city. But if large, well-funded cities are struggling to pass the policies and plans they need to address climate change on the necessary timeline, then you can imagine how much larger the gaps are for smaller towns. Let this serve as a wake-up call for urgent local action from mayors, councils, boards, and commissions in all cities, towns, and communities across the country.

Local engagement is one of the most rewarding and impactful ways to create change. In many ways, state and local action is even more important than what the federal government does (or doesn't) do. The power of these "subnational" actors is a hallmark of our American democracy and federalism structure. Power is divided between the national government and the states. And since mayors and governors represent us locally, they should be more in tune with what our communities are experiencing and need than all of Congress or the President.

The example of the "We Are Still In" coalition from Chapter 1 showed the power of state and local leaders coming together to keep climate action moving forward even as the federal government was rolling things back under the first Trump term. I spoke with Elan Strait, the Founder and Campaign Manager of "We Are Still In," about this. He told me that his work opened a discussion about not waiting around for federal climate action. "We have a lot of power and agency in solving climate change. The [first] Trump Paris Agreement withdrawal forced us to think about what the role in our own communities can be in fighting climate change. I think it can be really empowering for people to think about what you, your neighbors, and your families and communities can do."

It is disheartening when national officials fail to be the leaders we need them to be. But we can harness the power of the grassroots to build movements that demand change. If you doubt that local and community engagement can enact change on a large enough scale, consider how they've been harnessed to change things for the *worse*.

Parental Activism

In 2021, parents and activists began showing up at local school board meetings in Loudoun County, Virginia with the intent to, as they put it, "end [the] racist and divisive ideologies infused into government schools."[4] These meetings were a pressure-relief valve for parents angry about school closings and Covid restrictions. Continuing today, school board meetings in Virginia and across the United States are flash points for the politics of diversity, equity, and inclusion, pronoun usage, LGBTQ rights, and culture-war concerns.

In 2022, "Fight for Schools," a Political Action Committee (PAC) formed in Loudoun County with the stated mission to "take back

America's schools." They ran attack ads against Democratic candidates in Virginia's 7th and 10th congressional districts with descriptions that included "The Radical Left has lost its mind."[5] Ian Prior, the group's executive director, told ABC7 News at the time, "I think we need to focus next year on electing school board members that will really reshape the process and empower the school board and the people to have more say in how things are done."[6]

A similar group, "Moms for Liberty" (M4L), has become one of the fastest-growing political organizations in history—growing in just a few short years to over 130,000 members across 310 chapters in 48 states.[7] M4L uses Facebook to organize chapter members and encourages them to: engage with town boards and commissions, get involved in elections, file lawsuits, and lead efforts to ban books in local libraries and schools. This has wreaked havoc in communities across the country in all sorts of intended ways, sowing deep divides and resentments between neighbors that were not there before. The group has also become very influential within the national Republican Party.

This new brand of "parental activism" has unleashed a wave of political energy at every level of government. To be sure, many of these efforts are fueled and organized by well-funded national interest groups that have a lot to gain from co-opting the energy and anger of the grassroots for their own political advantage. But that doesn't dismiss the sentiments that led to these movements and that are still causing many parents to remain very locally active. Even if you disagree with the goals of groups like M4L, as I do, there's a powerful lesson in how quickly a personal issue can become a political movement. Once something feels personal, people show up. They stay involved. They organize. They demand change. We should see this as empowering.

What if the climate movement built our organizing and communications approaches in the same direct, local, vocal, and family-values-driven ways? What if we harnessed the same energy for good? Moms—and dads—should be just as concerned about climate threats as they are about books.

We have an incredible opportunity to come together and get things done locally. Rather than constantly focusing on national climate policies that are failing to pass (or that one administration is passing and another is rolling back), or focusing on the international climate negotiations that happen so far removed from most of our daily lives, we should redirect our attention to community and local engagement that can have a more direct impact on our lives. This refocusing also shifts public pressure to state and local leaders who, again, often have much more power than federal legislators to either support or prevent the most important climate programs from reaching us.

* * *

It's one thing to *recognize* the need to do something at the community level. It's another thing to know *how*.

Let's do a quick exercise. You live in a state that has different regions or "districts" associated with the territories of federal and state representatives. Those districts are made up of counties, and your town is in one of those counties. Look up and write down the answers to the following:

- Who is your US House of Representatives congressperson and which federal district are you in?

- Who are your US Senators? (Every state has two.)

- Who is your Governor?
- Who is your State Delegate and State Senator? (Most places have one of each).
- What county are you in?
- Search for your county's government structure. They should have a website. List some of your county's boards and commissions.
- What town do you live in?
- Write down your Mayor.
- Write down your Town Council members.
- If you live in a larger city, you may have additional local governmental subdivisions including Wards, Aldermen, or Advisory Neighborhood Commissions. Note these if you do.
- Search for your town's government structure. They should have a website. List some of your town's boards and commissions.

My example (in Spring of 2025):

I live in the beautiful Shenandoah Valley town of **Front Royal, Virginia**. That's in Virginia's **6th congressional district.** My US House representative is **Ben Cline (R)** and my two US Senators are **Tim Kaine (D)** and **Mark Warner (D)**. The Governor of Virginia is **Glenn Youngkin (R)**. My Virginia House of Delegates representative is **Delores Oates (R)** and my State Senator is **Timmy French (R)**. The Mayor of Front Royal is **Lori Cockrell**. Front Royal is in **Warren County**.

Front Royal has an elected Town Council and local governmental departments that include **Community Development & Tourism, Energy Services,** and **Public Works.** Front Royal has town boards and commissions that residents can join, and that hold public meetings for the public to provide input. These include the **Advisory Committee for Environmental Sustainability,** the **Planning Commission, Board of Zoning Appeals,** and others. Warren County also has county boards and commissions including the **Anti-Litter Council, Parks & Recreation Commission, Board of Building Code Appeals** and more. The Warren County **Board of Supervisors,** made up of five elected representatives (one from each of the county's five magisterial districts), directs policies for county affairs and county governmental departments and has the power to appoint individuals to the various county boards and commissions.

This may seem like a lot, with many redundant names of overlapping representatives, departments, and boards—as you can see in my example. But keep in mind that these increasingly smaller divisions of government are designed to present more access to you and more accountability. These divisions may have different goals, but they are still responsible to you—and a combination of these places may be where you need to go to discuss local climate solutions.

From health services to housing to energy to public works, making the places we live truly resilient to climate change and addressing the needs of everyone in the community will involve every level of decision-making. But once you make your list, I hope navigating where to go and who to go to will start to feel more manageable. You may even gain a deeper connection to your community by understanding and engaging in the process of how decisions are made that affect you and your family. The information is out there; it just takes a few minutes on your favorite search engine. Print out your list and any contact information you find, and pin or tape it where you can see it.

Congratulations—you're now better prepared to engage with your elected officials than most Americans! Nearly every person on your list is someone you could be talking to about your climate change concerns.

I know we don't always feel like politicians listen to us. But think about where you live and ask yourself—who are the loudest voices an elected official might hear in your community, and on what issues? If you live in a rural area, are they hearing more from farmers who might be resistant to land or water use changes that could be perceived as making things harder for them and their livelihoods? Are there oil, gas, coal, timber, or other extractive industries in your area? What are their interests, and are they being heard more than those advocating for climate solutions?

There's nothing wrong with a group of people sharing a common goal and making their voices heard to the officials that represent them. This is, in fact, a superpower all of us hold. We live in a representative democracy—every official is elected by us. We, as their voters, are their constituents, and responding to constituent concerns is one of the main jobs elected officials have. If they don't, we can vote for someone who will.

In many of the ugly school board fights that gained national attention, constituents associated with Moms for Liberty were the loudest voices in the room—not necessarily the majority, but the loudest—and so local elected officials acted accordingly.

In my area, local activists from Moms for Liberty and other conservative religious groups successfully influenced the Warren County Board of Supervisors to take action over books they wanted removed from Samuels Public Library. Samuels is an independent non-profit organization but relies on county funding to survive. The library is beloved in the community, provides critical resources, is Virginia's second oldest library (established in 1799), and has received numerous awards for excellence, including Virginia's Library of the Year award in 2024.

In March of 2025, after a multi-year fight where many in the community passionately and repeatedly spoke out in support of the library during public meetings that drew national media attention—including coverage by *Last Week Tonight* with John Oliver—the County Board of Supervisors voted not to renew the library's funding.

The fight continues as the library struggles to survive on donations alone. But there are many engaged community members, including me, who are not going to let a small group of ideologically driven politicians carrying out orders from extreme and well-funded national anti-LGBTQ groups get away with this.

"Just Show Up"

The Samuels Public Library example highlights community organizing and engagement at its best and worst. Many times, engagement is needed from all of us just to counteract the bad actors seeking change for their own personal or ideological benefit—the Newtonian Rule of Politics at work again. But if this level of engagement is needed to keep books in public libraries, it is needed even more so on local climate and clean energy-related fights.

What work do you need to do to build a "climate constituency" in your town? What public meetings may be occurring right now that seek input on projects or policies that could impact how your town deals with climate or environmental concerns? Keep in mind you may easily be able to piggyback your interests with different groups and constituencies in your town, or use them as a stepping stone to forming your own group.

In other not-so-high-profile fights, especially at the very local levels, you might find yourself one of the *only* voices in the room. Let's return to Elan Strait—after "We Are Still In," he worked on a campaign to pass a clean energy standard in Michigan. There were a small number of state legislators on the fence that his campaign needed to convince. These legislators held "coffee hours" in their districts that anyone could attend and raise important issues.

As Elan explained to me, "the difference between three people or five people coming to these coffee meetings, and two of those people coming in talking about climate change, made all the difference. These are local legislators who only need a few thousand votes to win their elections, and they are very responsive to local input. And the difference between Michigan getting a clean energy standard can help tip the balance as to whether or not the entire US is able to pass a clean energy standard."

The best thing anyone can do personally to advocate for and make a difference on climate change in their community? "Just show up," he said.

Thanks to Elan's and many others' efforts, in November of 2023, Michigan signed into state law a "Clean Energy & Climate Action Package," which included a 100 percent clean energy standard.[8] This means that by 2040, Michigan has committed to produce 100 percent of its electricity from clean sources. There are also interim benchmarks and milestones along the way to assist in the transition away from fossil fuels to renewable energy sources. There are currently twenty-four states, plus the District of Columbia and Puerto Rico, with 100 percent clean energy goals/standards.[9]

Continuing on to make positive change and find new ways to speak to climate audiences, Elan is now the Chief Program Officer for the Potential Energy Coalition. Potential Energy is the organization that partnered with the Yale Program on Climate Change Communications on the study mentioned in Chapter 7 of 60,000 people across twenty-three countries that showed how popular the dual messages of urgency and protecting the next generation are. They are doing important work, using data to help shift the narrative on climate change, find messages that appeal across ideological divides, and increase support for policy solutions.

These and other positive stories of local climate action transforming communities are out there, despite the lack of national media attention in many cases. These stories get lost among the national noise and punditry, even in the communities where they happen. This affects our perception of what we think is happening, often for the worse. It is important for us to learn and tell these stories to counter the popular opinion many have that "nothing has been done" on climate change. Vital work *has* been done that can provide best practices and case studies we may be able to implement elsewhere. Telling these stories gives us hope. It keeps our positive vision for the future strong and gives us something tangible to work toward.

Of course, more work than ever still needs to be done. And we can't stop at passing a new commitment or policy. How those policies are implemented is just as important. Staying engaged with your local officials can keep you involved in how things are being run in your community. You can help raise awareness if further changes need to be made. But multiple things can be true at once—we can recognize the urgent work we still need to do, soberly face the increasing threat of climate change each year, and celebrate the progress we've already made all at the same time. We must do this to keep ourselves motivated.

Build Community

I realize at this point I've spent a lot of time talking about the "who," "what," and "where" of local engagement, but there are still some missing pieces on the "how." I've outlined generally what engagement with elected officials, commissions, boards, councils, and so on can look like. As with the parental activism example, this can happen through outreach you individually engage in or collectively alongside a group you're part of. This is "issue education" or "direct policy advocacy." It can take shape in many ways but may include: writing a letter, making a phone call, or sending an email to your officials' offices. You could also request an in-person meeting or attend a public hearing. Direct engagement with your officials is possible at all levels of government. But it can be more convenient and effective close to home.

As with most issues, there are also like-minded groups you can think about joining on this journey. The Climate Reality Project (CRP), founded in 2006 by former Vice President Al Gore, has trained a global network of over 3.5 million passionate climate advocates. Chances are a local CRP chapter may exist not far from you.[10] Volunteers engage in local climate policymaking, organize protests and marches, and train others to conduct *Inconvenient Truth*–style PowerPoint presentations to their communities on the latest climate science and impacts.

Citizens Climate Lobby (CCL) is another great example of a grassroots network of local chapters across the United States committed to advocating for federal carbon tax legislation.[11] CCL volunteers are given the tools to engage with state and local elected officials in their areas, and many even participate in annual fly-ins to lobby their federal representatives in DC. They've also launched a new initiative to have more "open and honest conversations with their friends, family, and communities about climate change."[12] Since April 2024, CCLers have logged over 42,000 climate conversations in all fifty states. "Connect on a personal level," is their Step One in how to start these conversations.

There are also numerous national environmental organizations with local chapters as well as many state and local groups that may already be operating in your community. There are so many pathways for engagement—all it takes is a few internet minutes to find them.

At the most basic level, you or the group you're part of are attempting to influence a policy decision your officials are making. Building a new park, creating bike lanes, improving public transportation, requiring buildings to be more energy efficient, creating a recycling program, banning single-use plastics, and passing a city-wide greenhouse gas emissions reduction target are all examples of policies that you may champion in your town and therefore influence officials to support them.

The only real barrier may be the false belief that you have to know a lot about whatever issue you're advocating for. You may feel intimidated by those who "know more" than you. Reject that premise. You know your concerns, and you know what is important to your family and community. Share your story, your concerns, and your wishes for the future with your elected officials. It's as simple as that. Make your voice heard. Use your superpower.

You must be persistent in this type of direct engagement. But always be respectful, honest, and maintain your integrity. Local engagement in many parts of the country may mean that you have to interact with people who think very differently from you. If you become belligerent or untrustworthy, your voice can much more easily be ignored, despite all your great work. Be empathetic. Understand the range of issues facing the community. Don't underestimate personal connections and references. Be gracious. Be kind. Even if you ideologically disagree with your elected officials, these people have committed to a career of public service, and you should thank them for taking the time to speak with you.

Another great source of support is from your county political party committee. Most counties have organizations of local volunteers who are dedicated to the Democratic or Republican party principles. Most have websites and social media channels where they keep people updated with local events and meetings. If you sign up to volunteer with your county party, you may find like-minded individuals in your community who may already be engaged in the exact climate issue you are interested in. They can help you navigate your local elected officials, boards, commissions, and make it easier for you to learn more about the issues.

I've worked across the country at national levels of politics and policymaking and, let me tell you, I love local county parties! They are filled with some of the most dedicated changemakers I've ever met. Some of these people know *everything* that has happened in their community over the past fifty years. As such, they can be a little stressed out, sometimes a little wild, often a whole lot of fun, and always eager to help.

Even if you're not political at all, you can still get involved in community education on the science and impacts of climate change. You can get involved in helping to steer the implementation of local infrastructure projects. You can grab a shovel, pull some weeds, recycle plastic litter, and help beautify your city or clean up a river. You can help empower the next generation to have a stronger connection within the natural world and become better stewards of our shared resources. These grassroots and educational actions can have a huge impact when taken repeatedly over time by many people.

Each of us has agency. Each of us can make change and build community.

2,400 years ago, Aristotle said that the partnership that enables us to achieve our highest collective good is that to our community. "Polis" (city-state) is how Aristotle would have referred to it. And he saw this polis—the root word of "politics"—as much more than a form of governance. It is a collection of human beings, drawn together by our nature, in a fundamental arena that creates connections and enables us as individuals and communities to thrive.

Let us then end with a new and simple call-to-action for climate activism that puts more pressure on local and state elected officials than ever before. It is no longer acceptable for any leader to be caught unprepared by extreme heat, storm, flood, or fire. The foundation of our politics should be the safety of our polis—our communities. Without this protection, our government has failed in its basic duty—guaranteed to us by the Declaration of Independence—to secure our unalienable rights of "Life, Liberty, and the pursuit of Happiness."

10

How to Enact Change at the Federal Level

This book is coming out in a political environment that is the most "anti-federal government" in modern memory. Some of this backlash is targeted at the executive branch and federal agencies. For instance, a February 2025 Executive Order directed every newly confirmed agency head to prepare large-scale reductions in force (RIF) to their own agency's workforce. One month later, 50,000 confirmed cuts had been made, 75,000 buyouts had been taken, and 200,000 more immediate reductions were planned. At the US Agency for International Development and Voice of America, 99 percent of employees had been fired. Nearly 50 percent of employees were fired from the Department of Education. At the time of this writing, it was projected that cuts to the federal workforce could grow to upwards of 2.4 million people over the following years.[1]

Countless federal employees moved to encrypted messaging platforms like Signal—terrified to say the wrong thing about what was going on lest they give any reason to be targeted for cuts and "RIF'd," as they referred to the process. Yard signs declaring "We Support

Federal Workers" popped up alongside "Black Lives Matter" and "In This House, We Believe."

Alongside these executive actions, a new majority in Congress also targeted their legislative branch power against the federal government. Congressional Republicans marched in lockstep with actions that even sought to remove oversight from them in Congress—a core component of our constitutional system of checks and balances. These lawmakers targeted laws for repeal to satisfy the will of the President, including many related to the environment, clean energy, and climate change.

As Texas Republican Congressman Michael Cloud put in a press release in March of 2025,

> Republican lawmakers who are jubilant about President Trump's flurry of executive orders and actions reshaping the government are staring down a challenge: making those changes last by turning them into law. For now, the GOP majorities in Congress are largely happy to cede power to the executive branch as Trump tests the limits of his executive authority. But as court challenges and future elections threaten to undo those actions, these lawmakers are strategizing about how to cement them into legislation and then law.[2]

This book calls for federal action as a pillar in facilitating the institutional changes needed to solve climate change. There are many ways citizens can engage with federally elected officials, either individually or collectively, using the same strategies I presented in the previous chapter. But, you're probably wondering, how in the world can we enact *change* at the federal level with a congressional majority "happy to cede power" to a hostile administration and with federal agencies fighting for their very survival?

We *can* still make change at the federal level on important issues. But, just like making change at personal or community levels, it requires: knowing our audience, knowing our "why," effectively communicating how these policies and programs actually help the people they intend to help, and knowing our positive vision for where we are headed. Taking these steps can enable us to build grassroots efforts that trickle up to national decisions.

Challenges face us today as they have at times in the past and might again four, eight, or twenty years from now. "Institutional renewal is a task that faces every generation anew," Derek Thompson and Ezra Klein write in their book *Abundance*. They argue, "You can't expect all the institutions and laws and bills and processes from 40 years ago or 50 years ago to fit the moment you're in."[3]

This is the case for environmental laws just as it is for housing, zoning, or immigration laws. The public becomes frustrated with stagnation and bureaucracy when it seems like we can no longer solve big challenges.

Both Democrats and Republicans agree we are long overdue for institutional renewal, especially related to the federal government. But to take up this generational task in a genuine way, we have to still believe our institutions are worth fighting for. They are. But polling on this is bleak. From my first few political campaigns more than fifteen years ago, the slogans of "Politics Is Broken," "Congress Is Broken," and "Government Has Failed" have only grown in popularity. People hear these things enough times, over enough years, and you wind up with a group in power dedicated to burning the system down. So here we are. Maybe things will swing back in midterms or the next presidential election. But we also need to make a new case for federal policymaking and regulation *in general*, to our frustrated audience of Americans who clearly don't see how these things are working for them today.

* * *

I began writing this chapter before the 2024 elections and am finishing some months into Trump's second term. So much is continuing to change, and it can be unclear one day to the next which policies we'll still have in place to advance our climate and clean energy goals. Decades of consensus over how we think about mercury pollution, clean air, or wastewater regulations are being erased overnight. As EPA Administrator Lee Zeldin said in 2025 when he announced dozens of historic actions to dismantle EPA regulations, "Today is the greatest day of deregulation our nation has seen. We are driving a dagger straight into the heart of the climate change religion."[4]

This contemptuous language exemplifies how perceptions of some of the actions we've tried to take to address climate change in recent years have become toxic and polarized with certain audiences. This is another example of how the issue of climate change and how we address it has become separated from the objective scientific reality of global warming and the threats we face. To lower emissions and stabilize warming, keeping our existing federal laws intact would certainly help. We also need new ones, such as putting a price on carbon to incentivize markets and industries toward decarbonization, or ending the more than $700 billion the United States spends each year on fossil fuel subsidies, including direct tax breaks and implicit subsidies that harm public health and the environment.[5]

But we are pretty far away from those new sweeping federal policies at the moment.

Now is the moment for us to double down on building our engagement and enacting change at the personal, local, and community levels, which can strengthen our movements for national change. Our individual and collective actions can open federal "policy windows" where the momentum and public support throughout the country crescendo and national action becomes inevitable. Think of all the actions we see in the first one hundred days of any new presidential administration. Many of these are the result of the policy windows that open up when voters head to the polls and, with their votes, tell those in power what they want them to do.

I have learned a lot about what works to make change at the federal level over many years. And yet, the world has changed, politics has fundamentally changed, and what worked in advocacy until now may no longer be enough. So, as we rebuild and reframe our movements, let's take a step back and make sure we are addressing the fundamental question of: "*Why* is federal action still important?"

It has become clear that before we can move forward on enacting change at the federal level, there is an immense need to communicate the Why to many skeptics. The simple answer is that there are just some things we cannot solve at individual or community scales. When you have concerns that cross state borders—pollution, climate change, interstate commerce, national security—a national structure is needed to address them. This is the classic tragedy of the commons scenario where people act in their own self-interest and deplete shared resources, which harms the common good. One state cannot burn all the coal it needs for power and pollute its rivers without affecting the downwind and downstream air and water quality of neighboring states. If there were no other reason for the federal government to exist *besides* minimizing environmental and climate harms to the public, that alone would be reason enough. But there are a lot more we will now explore.

The Business Case for Climate Policymaking

Federal actions to address climate and environmental harms should be recognized as important even if you're coming from the perspective of a "businessman" President, a Silicon Valley tech billionaire, or an entrepreneur elected to Congress. These individuals should have some awareness that the public and private sectors are not engaged in a zero-sum game—especially when they have received billions of dollars in federal government contracts, loans, subsidies, and tax credits that benefited their businesses.

In the climate movement, it is recognized that there are not enough public sector funds (i.e., government spending) to meet our global climate goals. The technological innovations and infrastructural overhauls required for a transition from the current fossil-fuel dominant energy mix to one of clean energy sources will require tens to potentially hundreds of trillions of dollars of investment over the next few decades. Only the private sector has a well that deep.

As then-US Secretary of State John Kerry delivered in a speech to the UN climate conference in Morocco in 2016,

Now, I've said many times, and I'll say it again today: It is not going to be governments alone, or even principally, that solve the climate challenge. The private sector is the most important player. And already we are seeing real solutions coming from entrepreneurs and academia. It's going to be innovators, workers, and business leaders, many of whom have been hammering away at this challenge for years who are going to continue to create the technological advances that forever revolutionize the way that we power our world.[6]

I was there in Morocco and saw Kerry give these remarks to a hungry crowd. President Trump had just been elected for the first time a few days earlier, and many at the climate conference were raw with concern about continued US leadership in this space. We choked up as Kerry described signing the Paris Agreement on behalf of President Obama and the United States earlier that year, on Earth Day, holding his two-year-old granddaughter, Isabelle.

He described joining millions of others on the first Earth Day in 1970, meeting his wife Teresa at the first UN climate conference in Rio in 1992, and thinking about the future his granddaughter would inherit as he waited for his turn to sign this historic new climate agreement. When it was time, he scooped his granddaughter up and brought her on stage to share in the moment.

There are few people in the world who have done more to advance climate policy solutions than John Kerry—a lifelong public servant of more than fifty years. And here he was, talking about the private sector as the most important player—a plea to the incoming Trump Administration to consider the business case for climate and clean energy policies. His crucial point was that as important as the private sector is, government leadership is still essential. Government plays an important role in partnering with the private sector, passing incentives to help them expand and grow nascent industries, taking on risk to seed and incubate innovative solutions that the private sector can then scale to market.

To this latter point, public research and funding through the Advanced Research Projects Agency-Energy (ARPA-E) led (as of 2022) to the formation of 129 new companies and hundreds more public-private partnerships that have brought many new and important technologies into products sold in the market today.[7] ARPA-E's mission is "to advance energy innovations that will create a more secure, affordable, and sustainable energy future for the entire United States."

This is just one example of how the government and the private sector can work together to the benefit of everyone with an excellent track record of success. But it's also worth noting that President Trump sought to eliminate ARPA-E during his first term, and the Heritage Foundation's "Project 2025" also called for getting rid of it. At the time of writing, the agency still exists.[8]

* * *

Let me highlight another example of why federal action matters, this time from a private sector perspective. In Bill Gates's book, *How to Avoid a Climate Disaster*, he thinks a lot about industrial sectors that are heavily reliant on fossil fuel manufacturing processes. These sectors are referred to as "hard-to-abate"—meaning their greenhouse gas emissions are hard to reduce. For example, the global production of plastics, steel, and cement. Concrete is the second most widely used material after water. If the cement and steel industries were a country, it would be the world's third-largest emitter of greenhouse gas emissions. By most estimates, steel and cement production account for just over 50 percent of global industrial sector emissions.[9] And future emissions from these sectors are expected to significantly increase as the world grows.[10]

Currently, it is too expensive to produce low or zero-carbon plastics, steel, or cement. Capturing and storing emissions from these sectors could raise product prices by 25 percent or more. This is also true for jet fuel—the cost of switching to advanced biofuel alternatives is much higher than the current carbon-intensive jet fuel option. The difference in cost between a product that involves emitting carbon and an alternative that doesn't is what Gates calls a "Green Premium."

Green Premiums are too high for most products today because both the carbon-intensive and non-carbon-intensive manufacturing options still exist. But, as Gates points out, we can use new public policies to create incentives or mandates to produce or buy zero-carbon cement, steel, and other products. We can put a price on carbon. These and other federal policy actions would level the manufacturing playing field, making cheap, carbon-intensive alternatives less readily available, and lower Green Premiums for clean products. These actions would also drive down emissions.

"Lowering Green Premiums is the single most important thing we can do to avoid a climate disaster," Gates writes. To do this, "There are two levers that governments can pull: reduce the cost of zero-carbon alternatives or charge for the hidden costs of pollution. Ideally, any plan to address climate change does both."[11]

Here's an example Gates provides in his book:

> Suppose you're an engineer working for the city of Seattle, and you're reviewing bids to repair one of our many bridges. One bid comes in charging $125 a ton for cement, and another comes in charging $250 a ton, having added on the cost for carbon capture. Which one will you pick? Without some incentive to opt for the zero-carbon cement, you'll go with the cheaper one.
>
> ... Or, if you run a car company, will you be willing to spend 25 percent more on all the steel you buy? ... In an industry with narrow profit margins, a 25 percent premium could be the difference between staying in business and going broke ... at these prices we'll never drive the kind of system-wide change we need to get to zero. Nor can we count on consumers to drive down the prices by demanding more of these green products. After all, consumers don't buy cement or steel—large corporations do. ... Businesses are much more likely to pay the premium for clean materials if the law requires it, their customers demand it, and their competitors are doing it.[12]

For the industries and sectors where clean alternatives still aren't cheap enough yet and policy mandates would increase product costs too much, innovation is needed. Gates believes this is another area where governments around the world can lead. He calls for a quintupling of clean energy and climate-related publicly funded research and development over the next decade. Similar to the ARPA-E model, governments can develop breakthrough new clean technologies and partner with the private sector to deploy them within their manufacturing processes. There is money to be made in the clean industrial revolution.

Making Government Work Better

We have to rebuild public trust and buy-in for the institutions of government. That starts with ensuring they are more effective. And I'm not talking about a Department of Government Efficiency that has so far sought only to dismantle the government.

If we believe the government has a role in solving climate change, then we must make government work better, faster, and more fairly, reducing the influence of special interests that block change—even from our own side.

Not In My Backyard Democrats have effectively blocked housing affordability policies in Democratic cities across the country—which have now become the most expensive places to live. This is driving working-class people out of these areas. President Biden's historic Bipartisan Infrastructure Law included $42 billion to bring rural broadband to 25 million Americans currently without high-speed internet access. But by the time Trump was sworn in again more than three years later, the program had yet to connect virtually anyone, due to delays and bureaucratic red tape. There are many examples like these; bureaucracy will have to change if we are to have any hope of utilizing our institutions toward solving climate change.

The days of patient acceptance of government processes and public works projects progressing at a snail's pace as we throw billions of dollars at them with little return on our investment are over in America. And that's not a bad thing.

To stay on track with emissions reductions, the sheer scale of clean energy deployment, resilience infrastructure, public transport, projects that make buildings more efficient, and many other physical solutions to climate change will need to be built out at a much more rapid pace than our current system allows.

These examples help provide a better Why for the role of the federal government in combating climate change and show why the business community and markets are likely to respond favorably. The low cost of wind and solar—driven, in part, by federal, state, and even sometimes local government tax credits—provides even more examples. But whether it's incentives for renewable energy, ending fossil fuel subsidies, lowering Green Premiums, improving industrial manufacturing policies, state-based 100 percent clean energy standards, or any other idea, again, I am not advocating for one over the other.

I have written this book to offer a lens through which we can look at all the best climate policy proposals, figure out how we can build the public support needed to pass them, and then go out and make change—from the national level down to what makes the most sense in our states, towns, and individual lives.

I also can't overstate the importance of knowing the Why for any individual policy solution we pursue. Our best advocacy messages and tactics fall apart if we can't clearly explain how these specific changes will help solve the problem and improve people's lives.

* * *

Taking all of this into consideration, the remainder of the chapter presents two lenses through which we can think about making change at the federal level, no matter what happens in the current or any future administration. I call these my "North Stars," and they continue to make the case for why federal action is needed, while also providing clear avenues for anyone to engage.

The first is the North Star of public lands conservation. As part of the public lands, public waters, and ocean conservation communities for many years, I believe this can be a path forward for bipartisanship, a way to renew our faith in government institutions, to show a clear role for the federal government, and a place to build community across generations. There are meaningful stories and case studies where local solutions have had national significance. I will share some.

But first, it's important to note that a series of executive orders on mining, timber, and other pro-extractive industry actions taken by the Trump Administration have raised the threat of selling off America's public lands. Some have even floated the idea of public land being used to create more affordable housing. Even as we desperately need more affordable housing, these are terrible ideas that threaten our national heritage of public lands and waters that are owned and enjoyed by all of us. We should continue to watch closely and be concerned about any executive or legislative proposals that would seek to privatize our shared public resources.

The Salmon Forest

One of the most personally meaningful campaigns I've participated in was in Alaska's Tongass National Forest. At 17 million acres, the Tongass is by far the largest national forest in the United States. Even though it's in Alaska, it gets so much rain between its coastal and mountainous habitat that it is actually considered one of the largest intact temperate rainforests in the world. The Tongass's 15,000 miles of rivers and 123,000 acres of lakes and ponds provide habitat for some of the world's largest and most productive wild salmon runs.[13] Once they're ready to spawn, salmon return home to the rivers of the forest and feed over fifty different animals, from black bears to bald eagles. After they die, their nutrients help fertilize the land and literally get absorbed back into the trees that once sheltered and provided their spawning habitat.

The salmon also support a thriving commercial fishing industry and a way of life for indigenous peoples in the area who have relied on the forest and all it provides for thousands of years. For these reasons, the Tongass is known as the "salmon forest."

The Tongass also has incredible climate value. Because of its high concentration of old-growth trees—some more than 800 years old—this one forest in Alaska sequesters 20 percent of the carbon held by the entire US federal forest system. This is the equivalent of keeping about a year and a half of the entire country's greenhouse gas emissions out of the atmosphere. The Tongass is quite literally the lungs of North America.[14] The value of so much pristine, ancient old-growth habitat is hard to quantify. It provides a haven for biodiversity, natural resistance to wildfire, and other ecological benefits that contribute to climate resilience.

I was part of a coalition that included conservation organizations, native Alaskan tribes, fishermen, scientists, and citizens from Alaska and across the country dedicated to keeping the Tongass protected against threats from clear-cut old-growth industrial logging. From the 1950s to the present day, more than one million acres of the Tongass have been clearcut.[15] Half of the forest's large old-growth trees were logged in the last century. But the Tongass, along with parts of other forests across the country, was mostly protected under the 2001 US Forest Service "Roadless Rule"—a federal policy that prohibited the building of roads and timber harvesting in specific areas of national forests designated as roadless. The Roadless Rule didn't protect everything, but it helped keep a lot of these timber operations from expanding.

When these old-growth trees are cut, habitat for salmon and other species is destroyed. The soil erodes and fills the streams salmon need to survive, hurting all who rely on the salmon, including humans. I flew in a small plane over parts of the Tongass and saw for myself the old clearcuts that still stretch like scars across the hills and mountains. Decades after the logging had stopped, not much had returned besides grasses and very small trees. It takes generations for these trees to become large and populated enough to once again support a thriving habitat. Many of the rivers and streams are never restored.

During the first Trump term, there was an effort to overturn the Roadless Rule in Alaska and open up more than half of the forest to logging. Our coalition fought for years against this, raising awareness in Washington and educating a new generation on the benefits of the 2001 rule—to nature and humans. We were unsuccessful, as protections for the Tongass were stripped in the final days of Trump's first term. But a change in administration, well aware of the grassroots and national fight that was happening, halted any lease sales from occurring and immediately started a new process to protect the forest again. President Biden fully restored Tongass protections in his term. But on Day One of his second term, President Trump once again stripped protections via executive action.

The fight for the Tongass continues. But it's an interesting case study for understanding how federal action can have big consequences from one administration to the next—and thereby, one election to the next. It also sheds light on the "staying power" of regulatory and executive actions across different federal regimes—aka: the longevity and security of these actions—and how we should think about the progress we make on the environment, on climate, or any other issue as time goes on. Are any of our "wins" truly set in stone? What work do we need to do across every new generation to keep the public aware of and connected to these important issues?

My work to help keep the Tongass protected was also particularly important to me given my time as a crab and salmon fisherman in Alaska and my deep respect for Indigenous communities I've gotten to know up there (and elsewhere). This work connected me to the spirit of the early days of the environmental movement—to the "tree huggers" fighting against deforestation. As challenging as it was, it was an inspiring experience grounded in grassroots activism.

No one president or industry should have the ability to ravage so many vast acres of resources we all rely on. Polling shows that Americans overwhelmingly agree, at least in support of our protected national parks. But not all public land is protected—in fact, most isn't. It's still very hard in some communities to designate new public lands as protected—just as it was hard to create many of our national parks when they were first protected. Extractive industries create a lot of opposition. Local Indigenous peoples, hunters, fishers, and sportsmen and women can be critical validators to communicate why these places should be conserved. A chorus of local voices that express the many benefits of protected public lands and waters to us now and for future generations goes a long way. A land made for you and me, as the classic folk anthem goes.

Conservation to Heal the Moment We're in

There are plenty of ways to get involved in conservation efforts near us within local coalitions and groups. For instance, many rivers have a local Riverkeeper organization. There are volunteer "friend groups" that conduct trail maintenance, run educational programs, and raise funds for local parks—for instance, there are over thirty state parks in Virginia with friend groups.[16] League of Conservation Voters has local affiliated chapters in at least thirty states. Additional organizations and groups are easily found online. And don't forget to make use of your local government cheat sheet you put together in the last chapter for many more potential opportunities for engagement in local boards, commissions, and town and county meetings for the purpose of conservation.

Many public land and water conservation efforts are federal in nature. Our largest land management agencies—the Bureau of Land

Management, Forest Service, National Park Service, and others—are federal agencies. Some efforts, like establishing a new national park or passing a wilderness bill, also require Congress. But local and community efforts can trickle up to national decisions, and many times there are avenues for local stakeholder engagement in federal land management decisions, particularly in the local counties and "gateway communities" near these lands.

As challenging as it can be to build these conservation movements at first and to educate new generations on their importance, there is a long tradition of bipartisan conservation work over our nation's history. President Ronald Reagan, for instance, signed many new wilderness bills into law.

Before Reagan, Republican President Theodore Roosevelt created the US Forest Service and 150 national forests. He designated five national parks, four national game preserves, and fifty-one federal bird reserves. He also signed the Antiquities Act into law in 1906, which enabled him to designate the first eighteen of our national monuments. For these actions, Roosevelt is often referred to as the "conservationist president."[17]

In 2000, Democratic President Bill Clinton protected 140,000 square miles of the Northwestern Hawaiian Islands Coral Reef Ecosystem Reserve, which he called "The Yellowstone of the Sea"—the single largest conservation area established in the United States at the time.

In 2006, Republican President George W. Bush used the authority granted to him under the 1906 Antiquities Act to turn the area into "Papahānaumokuākea Marine National Monument"—making it the first marine national monument and first ecosystem reserve in the United States, setting a new global standard for coral reef and wildlife protection.[18]

President Obama then quadrupled Papahānaumokuākea to nearly 600,000 square miles—about four times the size of California. It is now one of the largest marine protected areas in the world and has gained status as the first marine World Heritage Site.

Even President Trump signed the largest land conservation legislation in a decade into law in 2019—a bipartisan effort sent to him by Congress in the first few months of his first term. This was a package of multiple conservation bills that protected more than two million acres of public lands and rivers across Utah, Oregon, California, and New Mexico.[19] But later in his term, he ordered a review of twenty-seven land and marine national monuments that ultimately opened millions of acres of protected public lands to industrial extractive development. In Utah, Grand Staircase-Escalante and Bears Ears national monuments were slashed by 50 percent and 83 percent, respectively. This was described by the Southern Wilderness Utah Alliance as the "single greatest attack a president has ever launched against America's federal public lands."[20]

President Biden restored these protections. But then, in Trump's second term—as part of his "Unleashing American Energy" Executive Order to dramatically expand domestic fossil fuel production, mining, and other extractive activities on federal lands—he once again directed the departments of Interior and Agriculture to "reassess any public lands withdrawals for potential revision." This could open up protected national monuments or any other form of protected lands or waters.[21] And in April 2025, Trump did just that when he signed a proclamation to open up the protected Pacific Remote Island Marine

National Monument to commercial fishing—going against the bipartisan efforts of previous presidents.

As Angelo Villagomez, Senior Fellow at the Center for American Progress, said in the media at the time,

> President Trump is threatening to open public lands and waters to oil drilling deep-sea mining and industrial fishing and like a lot of things that have happened during the last 100 days the legality of this action is questionable . . . If you can open up the Pacific Remote Island Marine National Monument what's to stop him from opening up Yellowstone to uranium mining.[22]

Beginning with Roosevelt, nine Democratic and nine Republican presidents have each used the Antiquities Act to establish or expand protected areas of public lands and waters across the country. For over one hundred years, it has been widely accepted that the Antiquities Act grants power to the president to protect some of our most meaningful lands, waters, landmarks, and areas of scientific, historic, or ecological importance in areas controlled by the federal government. But there is also widespread acceptance that a president cannot single-handedly overturn these protections—only Congress has that power.

Despite the whipsaw of recent presidential administrations, there are additional bipartisan conservation examples at the congressional, state, and local levels we can point to. They were highlighted in my conversation with Ken Rait, who has worked for more than thirty years as a conservation professional, political strategist, lobbyist, and campaigner. Among the many organizations he has worked for, he directed conservation efforts at the Southern Wilderness Utah

Alliance. He also ran the Heritage Forest Campaign that successfully advocated for the initial creation of the 2001 Roadless Rule.

Ken told me about how, when he was starting in the 1980s working in Arizona for the Sierra Club, Democrats and Republicans had, earlier in the decade, teamed up to designate over 1.1 million acres of public national forest lands near the Grand Canyon as wilderness. This designation, in 1984, created the majority of wilderness areas around the Grand Canyon that millions of people enjoy today. Then, later in the decade, the Arizona congressional delegation wanted to honor Congressman Morris "Mo" Udall, who was suffering from Parkinson's. Mo was a leading conservationist and advocate for environmental protections, and Mo's older brother, Stewart, was instrumental in advocating for the 1964 Wilderness Act. Democratic Senator Dennis DeConcini and Republican Senator John McCain, as well as the rest of the Arizona delegation, came together in 1990 to designate another million acres of public land in Arizona managed by the Bureau of Land Management and the US Fish & Wildlife Service as wilderness.

"As has been said many times, wilderness is America's common ground," Ken told me. "Polling shows people across the political divide support land conservation. But issues around public lands are not top in voters' minds. How do you stay bought in, nationally? Everyone's so overwhelmed right now, which creates an opportunity for the current administration to seek to privatize public lands. A reboot and reinvention process is needed. Get away from your screen and out into nature. American politics isn't led so much by political leaders but by movements of people who can move those leaders. It's not infeasible that all sides of the political spectrum can come together to force leaders to be more conservation-minded. We've done this before. These are *our* public lands."

As for public lands solving the housing crisis? "That's not going to happen because of where many of these remote lands are located, without infrastructure, and where the economic development potential is limited," Ken said. "Where will people work? And is the government going to get involved to ensure those houses are built affordably? Of course not. Private developers would be used, to the benefit of large and wealthy landowners."

The Outdoor Recreation Economy

Even though we're talking about protecting nature, telling a story about the economic benefit of protected public lands and waters to local communities can also help—just as it can with climate solutions. There are those who believe conserving our resources harms economic development and kills jobs. The opposite is true. Protected areas bring more people to gateway communities near them, increase local tourism spending, and create an economy that relies on a flourishing natural environment rather than an extractive economy that destroys the environment.

But don't take my word for it. A peer-reviewed analysis conducted by economists at the National Park Service and US Geological Survey showed that, in 2022, that was "$23.9 billion of direct spending by more than 312 million park visitors in communities within 60 miles of a national park nationwide. This spending supported 378,000 jobs nationally," with over 300,000 of those jobs found in gateway communities. "The cumulative benefit to the US economy was $50.3 billion."[23]

Honing in on just one park, the Park Service analysis showed that spending by 4.7 million visitors to the Grand Canyon National Park in 2022 "supported a total of 9,990 jobs, $346 million in labor income, $576 million in value added, and $1.0 billion in [local] economic output."[24]

It's unclear who coined the term "outdoor recreation economy," but in 2012, the Western Governors' Association published its report "A Snapshot of the Economic Impact of Outdoor Recreation." They found that Americans spent $645 billion on outdoor recreation the previous year. As *Outside* magazine reported at the time, "Americans spend more money on outdoor recreation than they do on pharmaceuticals. More than on cars. More than on energy for their homes. . . . The point of the report was to say: Look, the recreation industry is an economic powerhouse."[25]

There is an economic value of conservation to the communities around protected areas and to the nation as a whole. This is an American industry just as important as any other. It even has its own industry association—the Outdoor Industry Association (OIA)—that publishes reports on outdoor participation trends and economic statistics. One OIA report from 2017 showed that, nationally, the outdoor recreation economy generates $887 billion in consumer spending, provides 7.6 million jobs, more than $65 billion in federal tax revenue, and nearly $60 billion in state tax revenue.[26]

This is spending from all forms of motorized and non-motorized outdoor recreation: hunting, fishing, camping, climbing, biking, motorcycling, water sports, snow sports, off-roading, and more.

Visitor dollars make their way into restaurants, hotels, gas stations, and all corners of the economy. But all of this relies on the places we love staying protected.

In Alaska's Tongass National Forest, over one million people visit each year onboard cruise ships.[27] Many of them take day trips into the forest to explore the amazing wildlife and habitat. They spend money on local guides, eat at local restaurants, and buy things from local businesses. Would as many tourists come if the forest they sailed, hiked, fished in, and kayaked through was all cut down?

Would as many people raft through the Grand Canyon on the Colorado River if new mines poured waste into its waters?

Front Royal, Virginia, where I live, is a gateway community to Shenandoah National Park—one of the main reasons my wife and I moved there. In 2023, our county brought in more than $87 million in tourism spending. Many of these tourists come for outdoor recreation at the national park, the Shenandoah River, three nearby state parks, and the Appalachian Trail. The dollars they spend benefit our local community.[28]

With such an important industry contributing jobs and revenue across the country—especially to rural and remote communities that don't have the same financial resources as urban areas—the least we can do is keep access to public lands and waters open and services funded. Trails need maintenance, safety railings along cliffs need to be replaced, bathrooms need to be cleaned, and roads and bridges need to be repaired. Park Rangers lead tours and educational programs. They also conduct rescues and perform emergency medical services on tons of people each year.

But mass federal layoffs by President Trump in 2025 led to thousands of National Park Service and US Forest Service terminations—5 percent and 10 percent of each agency's entire staff, respectively.[29] These terminations have already led to visitor center closures and a reduction in services. According to Emily Douce, deputy vice president of government affairs at the National Parks Conservation Association, "If it were a business, say like Disneyland or Disney World, if you had record-breaking visitation that brings in lots of money for the local economy, then you wouldn't be cutting staff.... You would be increasing the amount of staff to ensure visitors have a great time."[30]

Using all the tools this book provides, we must stand up and stand against these unprecedented attacks on our national heritage.

Environmental Justice

If housing affordability, rural economic development, and rising energy costs are important to you—as they are to most of us—then the lens of environmental justice provides another helpful framework for making change at the federal level.

This is my second North Star.

In recent years, anything that sounds related to "Diversity, Equity, and Inclusion" has become toxic with certain audiences. So using the term "environmental justice" may not be a great starting place with everyone. Instead of "DEI," some have suggested "Belonging, Dignity, and Justice" or even "Belonging, Dignity, and *Joy*" as better terms that focus more on universal values—and that are more centered in the experiences of marginalized people."[31] Instead of environmental justice, some would rather use "environmental *in*-justice" or "environmental racism," which they feel more accurately reflects what marginalized people have had to go through. I'm not suggesting one over another.

In our climate conversations, I think the most effective thing is to talk about specific programs that help people. If needed, we can avoid the too-high-level, generic, and sometimes polarizing debate about "environmental justice" and other labels altogether.

We are all experiencing the negative impacts from climate change. But as we work to empower personal and community change and rebuild our connections to one another, we cannot overlook the reality that not everyone is on the same level playing field. As climate advocates, it's important for us to keep in mind that some people we may be trying to reach may experience the impacts of warming far worse than we do. As we discuss solutions at any level of our engagement, there must be a thoughtful awareness of the significant socio-economic shifts that will come with a transition to green energy, shifts that will bring real changes to people's ways of life and work. This makes its way into our politics whether we like it or not. We know the increasing climate burden Americans feel contributes to their sense of institutional betrayal. More effective government programs that better protect us from climate hazards, and more effective communications about these programs, can restore our confidence in federal action.

This is what we mean when we talk about "equity." People are right to be skeptical of policies and plans they fear will make their lives harder. They are right to ask the question, "Is this fair?" It is the job of the creators of these plans to effectively address these concerns.

This is where we can, again, be thoughtful in our approach and communications. Climate solutions will fail if the transition to a clean energy economy does not happen in a just and equitable way for everyone, and it will fail if it is even perceived to be unequal.

Engagement in environmental justice can happen at all levels. It can begin with the deeply personal, as we strengthen our connections to those around us and increase our understanding of what they are going through. It can also be part of local engagement and community building.

Federal action can, once again, play a crucial role.

There is a decades-long awareness among some lawmakers that many communities across the country have experienced environmental injustice due to racial and/or socioeconomic disparities. This awareness is built on data. In 2012, for instance, it was found that six million people living within three miles of the United States's 378 coal-fired power plants had an average per capita income of just $18,400 per year. These low-income individuals were disproportionately minorities. Living so close to a coal plant, they were exposed to higher levels of mercury, lead, and other pollutants linked to asthma attacks, heart problems, and other diseases, all at much higher rates than the rest of the public.[32] There are many more examples of pollution and contamination affecting some communities worse than others. The people living in those communities are not to blame. Often, legacy decisions made decades or generations ago—by local officials no longer alive or companies no longer in existence—built an unsafe infrastructure for the people living there today.

The Biden Administration launched the most ambitious environmental justice agenda ever undertaken by the federal government to rectify some of this. They created the Justice40 Initiative, which was a meaningful and intentional approach to ensure 40 percent of the benefits associated with federal grants on housing, climate, and the environment went to support disadvantaged communities—especially as they rolled out historic new investments with the Inflation Reduction Act and Bipartisan Infrastructure Law. This was something every agency worked to weave into their grants and program designs as they sought to drive equitable outcomes with the new public funds Congress approved.[33] The Biden Administration also built a tool to identify environmentally unsafe communities and assess their needs. Key to their success was partnering directly with stakeholders in those communities to find solutions that worked for them. Alongside addressing legacy pollution, some of these programs also sought to address energy costs and energy transition needs, which also place a disproportionate burden on low-income and minority communities.

One such program designed to help is the State and Community Energy Programs (SCEP) at the Department of Energy (DOE). SCEP was created to "accelerate the development of innovative energy technologies to bolster communities, create jobs, save money, and strengthen energy independence and resiliency."[34] SCEP partners with communities across the country to provide resources and technical assistance.

I spoke with Chris Castro, who helped build SCEP and served as its inaugural Chief of Staff from 2022–2024. He also served as Director of Sustainability and Resilience for the city of Orlando, Florida. He told me how the Weatherization Assistance Program (WAP), which is part of SCEP, is the longest-serving low-income energy assistance

HOW TO ENACT CHANGE AT THE FEDERAL LEVEL 185

program in the United States. For 50 years, across Democratic and Republican administrations and different majorities in Congress, funding has been allocated to this program to increase the energy efficiency of low-income households. According to DOE,

> Through weatherization improvements and upgrades, these households save on average $372 or more every year according to a national evaluation of the program. Since the program began in 1976, WAP has helped improve the lives of more than 7.2 million families through weatherization services . . . the program supports 8,500 jobs and provides weatherization services to approximately 32,000 homes every year using DOE funds.[35]

Democrats and Republicans alike came together to create WAP as part of the 1976 Energy Conservation Policy Act, and continue to support the program today. Red and Blue states pull DOE funding down through Community Action Agencies or "CAAs." CAAs were created by the Economic Opportunity Act of 1964 and today form a national network of over 1,000 CAAs that serve virtually every county in the United States. You can find your local CAA using a tool on CommunityActionPartnership.com. Mine is the Skyline Community Action Partnership located just down the street from my home. Even though they're funded federally, CAAs are managed and means-tested by local county governments that reach out to homeowners based on local assessments of residents' needs. They provide upwards of thousands of dollars per household to improve weatherization, energy efficiency, indoor comfort, duct repair, enhanced insulation, HVAC improvements, and more.

Concerns over energy are pocketbook issues for voters. These simple upgrades not only directly save homeowners money, but they significantly improve climate resilience to extreme heat, cold, and other impacts for tens of thousands of homes each year. In 2024, Congress appropriated $360 million to this weatherization assistance program. The 2021 bipartisan infrastructure law signed by President Biden provided another $3.5 billion to the program on top of annual appropriations. And since this funding went to a program that has already been working well for so many years—with county-level implementation strategies and community relationships already in place—the money was quickly and efficiently distributed and is helping communities across the nation. As Chris described it, "Weatherization is a strategy to address environmental justice and empower some of our most disadvantaged and disenfranchised communities with resources that can improve their health and comfort, save them money, and more."

President Trump has, of course, sought to roll back President Biden's environmental justice actions. As part of his anti-DEI efforts, Trump terminated the Justice40 Initiative and canceled more than 400 grants to disadvantaged communities totaling $1.7 billion. This move has been viewed by some as illegal since funding was already approved by Congress under the Inflation Reduction Act. These are programs that were in the process of taking lead out of soil in Missouri, installing wastewater treatment systems in Alabama, building air quality monitors in North Carolina, and many more actions that would have helped communities across the nation reduce pollution and improve public health.[36]

Additionally, Biden's Climate and Economic Justice Screening Tool and the Obama-era Environmental Justice Screen and Mapping Tool have both been removed from government websites. These tools assisted home buyers and renters in making important decisions that affect the safety of their families when looking at where to live. They helped answer questions like, "How far away is my home from a hazardous waste site?" or, "How polluted is my neighborhood's air quality?" This is government-funded public data that belongs to all of us. Its removal has led to lawsuits and teams of volunteer researchers trying to recover it. You can find archived versions of both environmental justice screening tools as well as CDC health and environment resources, FEMA climate risk indexes, and other restored data on the website of the Public Environmental Data Partners. This organization describes itself as "committed to preserving and providing public access to federal environmental data." They have been referred to as "Data Heroes" by *Forbes*.[37]

These rollbacks come at the same time President Trump is trying to ramp up production of some of the dirtiest and deadliest sources of energy—like coal. Chapter 2 detailed how coal particulate matter 2.5 contributed to half a million deaths in the United States from 1999 to 2020 and how coal-fired power plants continue to be the largest source of toxic water discharges into our rivers and streams. If there was ever a need for data and programs that improve public health and the environment, that time is now.

There is some evidence that certain environmental justice ideas may continue under the branding of "cumulative impacts." The EPA under Trump has so far not removed its website on cumulative impacts research, which defines the issue as follows:

In everyday life, people can be exposed to numerous pollutants from a wide array of sources through multiple media and pathways. Chemical stressors in environmental media (air, water, land) and non-chemical stressors (e.g., social determinants of health, extreme weather events) aggregate and accumulate over time from one or more sources in the built, natural, and social environments, affecting individuals and communities in both positive and negative ways—referred to as cumulative impacts. In communities, particularly those already overburdened, disproportionate impacts can arise from unequal environmental conditions and exposure to multiple stressors. Additionally, changes in climate can exacerbate many of these disproportionate impacts.[38]

Similarly, the city of Washington, DC has gone from their Environmental Justice Amendment Act of 2023 to their Cumulative Impacts Analysis Amendment Act of 2025. This isn't exactly a rebrand, as the two bills have overlapping but not identical goals. Still, we could be seeing a shift in terminology that may have broader appeal to certain audiences. Other cities like Chicago and states like New York and Minnesota have also passed cumulative impact laws and ordinances. These require assessments and analyses similar to decades-old environmental reviews. But, as the Minnesota Pollution Control Agency describes it, "Cumulative impacts analyses can support arguments that environmental justice areas have faced disproportionate impacts from pollution and can provide new insights to address these negative outcomes."[39]

Thankfully, as of now, DOE's State and Community Energy Programs are still popular and operating. Weatherization assistance is just one of them. SCEP also has a program to help homes that don't meet the minimum standards of the weatherization program. You wouldn't improve a home's insulation or weatherstripping if there are large structural issues. So they started a Weatherization Readiness Fund as a new and separate fund to help get these homes improved so that they are ready for weatherization. Funds are also sent directly to states and counties. There was huge bipartisan support that came together to get this done in 2022.

There are additional programs like the Low Income Home Energy Assistance Program (LIHEAP), through the federal Health and Human Services agency, that provide further assistance with home energy bills, heating and cooling assistance, and weatherization to nearly seven million households. The Housing and Urban Development agency also provides federal funding to create community resilience in low-income areas. These and other programs are great examples of federal, state, and local government working together to help communities become safer and more resilient to climate-related impacts. Improving energy efficiency also helps reduce greenhouse gas emissions. It's plausible you could even expand these programs to middle-income households and include more projects to reduce emissions, like rooftop solar. Most importantly, these programs provide pathways for direct community engagement and are implemented at a local and county level.

I also spoke with Chris about his time as Director of Sustainability and Resilience for the city of Orlando, Florida. He told me how he managed a department that oversaw transportation, water, energy, building, local food systems, zero waste programs, and nature-based food systems. They worked with police and fire, the utility commission, and all other departments. The mandate was to integrate sustainability into all actions of the city. "We put Orlando on the map for an East Coast city leading on sustainability and resilience policies," he said.

Chris mentioned that in Orlando (as in other cities) many low-income individuals are renters—so not everyone directly benefits from weatherization or efficiency programs targeted at homeowners. So he worked with the public utility to create a new program that helped renters afford and install smart thermostats, better seal their doors and windows, and other efficiency upgrades that reduced their monthly utility bills. With these energy cost savings, the program pays for itself in just a few months. Chris's group also created a climate-smart housing program for seniors on a fixed income to improve the efficiency of their homes, using state funds and at no cost to the homeowner.

Orlando is at risk from hurricanes, extreme wind, and flooding. So the city created community resilience hubs to serve low-income areas often hit first and worst during a severe storm. Chris's team worked to retrofit six neighborhood centers to stock them with: ice, water, sand, a food pantry, and to enable them to be disconnected from the grid with backup battery power and decentralized energy with rooftop solar. They created solar-powered tables with backup battery power that they put into public parks so that people can charge their phones and stay connected in times of emergency. Additionally, they created mobile resilience hubs on wheels that provide similar services and can be moved into neighborhoods as needed.

* * *

Stories of communities becoming safer in the face of severe weather, or coalitions of people coming together to conserve our public resources, should fill us with hope. There is so much good work happening across the country, even as we gravitate toward negative news that makes us believe otherwise.

It's often overlooked how much federal funds, federal agencies, and federal laws 40–50 years old play in many of these success stories. But we all benefit nonetheless. It's plausible to see how these local programs and networks could expand to meet even more of our climate needs. Even if some federal funds are used to support these programs, they can still help to reduce the overall cost when disaster hits—which reduces the cost to us, the taxpayer. Another example of how investing in mitigating the impacts from climate change now can build resilience and reduce the much larger cost of adaptation, losses, and damages down the line. Let's advocate for these common sense ideas and ensure federal action remains strong.

I once had someone tell me that elected officials almost never change their stated positions—especially federally elected officials. But, this person suggested, maybe you can make that official, or their staff person, a champion on your issue because it is already in their self-interest. They may not know that taking the action you are suggesting is within their self-interest, but you can get them there. You may have to do the grassroots advocacy, build the community constituency, and/or mobilize voters to bring them along. Your work can help educate the elected official not only on the issue itself but also on the wide range of different voices coming together in support of the issue, which helps them see their political self-interest.

These are some of the tenets of grassroots mobilization, issue education, and direct policy advocacy core to this book, and that I went into detail on in Chapter 9. Remember that the same rules apply: be respectful, honest, and empathetic. Taking this critical step of direct engagement is something many of us skip—either out of ignorance of the process or apathy toward the system. But it can move mountains, or at least protect them. You can make change and change the system at the same time. And you are not alone.

CONCLUSION

There are seventy-three million of us in my Millennial generation, now the largest in the United States. Adding in Gen Z, we are 142 million strong. We are ages fourteen to forty-five, and we are certainly demanding many changes. Generation Alpha is also rising, with more than forty-two million and growing. They're projected to be the most racially and ethnically diverse generation in US history. Some are already reaching adolescence and starting to form their views on the issues that matter to them—even if they're still a few years away from full political participation.

But turnout data show that many young voters have become more conservative (Republican), at least in recent elections.[1] And research shows that Americans' partisan identities are stronger than race or ethnicity.[2]

Then there is the disengagement and apathy many young people feel toward the institutions of voting, political participation, and government. There is also the uncertainty they feel about their economic futures. A Harvard Youth Poll in April 2025 showed that: "More than 4 in 10 young Americans under 30 say they're 'barely getting by' financially, while just 16% report doing well or very well; Only 19% trust the federal government to do the right thing most or all the time."[3]

What does that mean for an issue like climate change—which requires broad public engagement, policy leadership at all levels, isn't always at the top of the list of voters' concerns, and has for so long has been coded as a liberal/progressive cause?[4]

Of course, it is not a bad thing to be conservative—as much as we divide ourselves into "my team" partisan mentalities. It's just that the politics of the Right have been mostly against climate solutions in recent years—if Trump's Executive Actions or Charlie Kirk's YouTube videos are any indication. As Edoardo Campanella and Robert Z. Lawrence wrote in a 2024 *Foreign Affairs* article titled, "The Populist Revolt Against Climate Policy: How the Culture War Subsumed Efforts to Curb Global Warming":

> Now, a new populist front is opening in Western politics. Anti-establishment leaders are singling out for scorn efforts to avert global warming. Attempts to curb climate change make an almost perfect target for populist rhetoric and conspiracy theories because policies to forcibly reduce carbon emissions rely on expert knowledge, raise costs for ordinary people, require multilateral cooperation, and rest on the hard-to-prove counterfactual that such policies would stave off disasters that would otherwise happen.[5]

All of this makes the case, more than ever, that we must figure out a path toward a Climate Activism 2.0. One that expands our messages to new audiences and builds bipartisanship. Policies *can* be crafted to provide economic incentives to make green technologies cheaper, to help people in the energy transition, to lower people's bills, to create clean energy economy jobs, and more.

But that all starts with the right messages, tactics, and engagement.

CONCLUSION

On these points, there are some things we can learn from movements on the Right. Craig Shirley has worked for the Republican National Committee, served as Communications Director for the National Conservative Political Action Committee, lobbied on behalf of the Heritage Foundation, has served under Presidents Reagan and George H. W. Bush, and has written six books on Reagan. *The American Conservative* places him at the "Very Top of Reagan Biographers."[6]

Craig told me he sees a lot of similarities between Reagan's 1980 and 1984 campaigns and Trump's 2016 and 2024 campaigns. Trump even used some of the same Reagan slogans, "Make America Great Again," and "Are you better off today than you were four years ago?" But more than that, Craig sees both Reagan and Trump as natural successors to preceding periods of political uncertainty, cultural anxiety, and economic hardship.

"The reason why they did so well," Craig explained, "is that, in both cases, they talked about a strong economic future for young Americans. Young people still want to believe in the future; in economic prosperity for them. The throughline was: optimism." In comparison, Craig describes the messages of Presidents Carter and Biden as being "downers" as the first navigated tough economic times during the 1970s and the second, recovery from the Covid-19 pandemic.

There are many differences between Reagan and Trump too, Craig acknowledged—especially on free trade. But there are important lessons from then to now. In 1980, conservatives were elated with Reagan's victory, which signaled the rise of a new conservative political movement based on limited government, deregulation, and anti-communism. "This was about restoring conservative ideas of individualism and the free market against collectivism," as Craig describes it. But he also said,

> today the politics are more personal. The victory of Trump's conservative movement has a bitterness in the wind to it. Decades of people feeling like they've been left behind, resentful of globalization and other changes, resentful of the elites and institutions that have failed them and left them behind; there's a politics coming from a deep place of resentment that is happy with Trump's victory but also bitter about the state of the world. For both Reagan and Trump, Make America Great Again meant American exceptionalism; a return to exceptionalism.

There are important points in Craig's analysis for anyone to take to heart. It's worth noting that this take on the MAGA movement is echoed by many others within, including Turning Point USA, which has these words on its website as part of its mission statement: "To empower informed civic and cultural engagement grounded in American exceptionalism and a positive spirit of action."[7]

Different partisan identities may carry different ideas for the future. But whatever you believe, you still have to believe in the future.

* * *

I first came to DC in the winter of 2008. The country was reeling in the wake of the global financial collapse, which threatened to rival the Great Depression. Friends I'd graduated college with the year prior were moving back in with their parents. I'd avoided a similar fate only by buying a one-way ticket to Dutch Harbor, Alaska, the month after I graduated and walking the docks until I got myself on a commercial crab fishing boat. I didn't even have a place to stay—I luckily met someone on the plane who let me crash for a few nights while I looked for work. I took huge risks and almost died so that I could make enough money to give myself options as I went out into the world in search of my career. To say young people in the years after 2008 felt anxiety about their economic future would be an understatement. The previous president had also sent many in my generation to war, including friends of mine. The country demanded change.

Then Barack Obama was elected and a wave of hope swept over young Democrats like me. I rode that wave to DC and became part of the Obama generation—motivated to make a difference and concerned that not enough was happening on important issues like climate change and equality. I can't tell you how great it felt to be young and in DC at that time—a place filled with smart, energized, and optimistic people. Everyone was alive and full of ideas. I think this spirit peaked on the evening of June 26, 2015, when the White House lit up with rainbow colors in celebration of marriage equality being upheld by the Supreme Court. Seeing the President openly celebrating this seemed radical; revolutionary. A grassroots victory after so many years. Love finally won.

Earlier in the day, I'd walked to the Supreme Court to celebrate with the crowd and had heard the Gay Men's Chorus of Washington sing "The Star-Spangled Banner." An incredibly moving moment. On my way home, I saw the White House lit up.

Obama inspired me more than anyone to get involved and make positive change. I entered my version of public service at first through political campaigns. I went out on the campaign trail, worked 100-hour weeks, and did my best to confront the anger of Tea Party activists and disinformation campaigns that talked of "Death Panels" in response to Obamacare. I came back to DC and marched alongside the Occupy Wall Street protesters. I wept as I watched Obama's helicopter fly over the city one last time from my apartment window on January 20, 2017. I entered the environmental conservation community and dedicated myself to something larger than myself. Now, I'm sharing the knowledge I've gained through these experiences to try and make the biggest impact against the threat of climate change I can. But all of this requires optimism. Staying engaged year after year requires hope for the future—no matter what is happening around you or who is in power.

I never met Obama, but I did meet Biden when he was Obama's Vice President. During a campaign event in Milwaukee in 2010, I saw Biden give one of the best and most energizing political speeches I'd ever seen. At twenty-six years old, I was absolutely fired up over it. "People are angry with good reason," Biden said as he talked about the devastation of the recession.

> If we let this remain a referendum on their anger, we will lose . . . When you're angry, you don't want to focus on the alternative. You only want to focus on your pain and your anger. And shame on us, shame on us if we let them do that, and not remind them of what the alternative is and the progress we've made.[8]

* * *

To Craig Shirley, Trump also symbolized change and the culmination of a years-long national movement. Change from eight years of the Obama Administration the first time around. Change from the Covid pandemic and inflation under the Biden Administration the second time around. Change from what conservatives saw as a buildup of the "Administrative State" under both Democratic presidents. On this latter point, Craig also mentioned Newton's Third Law of Politics as the equal and opposite reaction that led both Reagan and Trump to go after what they saw as a buildup of Big Government by their Democratic predecessors. "American Conservatism is about the individual over the state—always," Craig said.

These are the political realities we face right now. Young people are angry and anxious—on both the Right and the Left. They are worried about their economic futures; worried about their sustainable future. They need a hopeful vision from leaders who understand their experience, speak to them, and are willing to passionately fight for them.

The world has changed. Politics has changed. And so must we. We have to, if we're to solve the ticking time bomb of fossil fuel emissions. The Earth does not care about us; we must save ourselves. And to do that—to solve climate change and build a sustainable future that is both prosperous and hopeful—we must bridge our divides. Polarized partisan identities are paralyzing our ability to meet the moment and solve many of our big challenges. We have to turn our anger and anxieties into action.

This book offers tools to help build a climate voter who is more bipartisan, more personally connected to the issue, and more directly engaged in making change. Ask yourself, and ask others, "What does climate change mean to me/you, personally?" Ask—in the face of more frequent and severe climate disasters, "is my health, my allergies, the air I'm breathing and water I'm drinking better off today than it was four years ago?" Share those concerns with your local leaders and demand they better protect us.

Climate change isn't separate from the issues voters care about most—it is embedded in them. It will make immigration more difficult, inflation worse, and global instability more likely. The economic voter *is* the climate voter; as is the national security voter and the energy security voter. But we know greater issue identification is needed for many Americans, and generic majority support is not enough to translate into support for sweeping new policies. We need better communication strategies to close that gap.

The action steps throughout every chapter are designed to help you make those connections with others and show them how climate solutions link directly to things they care about. Every major societal challenge going forward will need to align with decarbonization and sustainability goals. We cannot continue to emit anywhere close to what we emit today if we wish to hold warming under two degrees Celsius and avoid meltdowns of our economic and geopolitical systems. The devastating consequences of climate failure would, without a doubt, affect every person on this planet regardless of what they say they care about. But transforming our global economy and fossil-fuel-based infrastructure will also affect everyone—for the better.

The solutions we advocate for need to be practical, effective, able to be implemented quickly, at a large enough scale, and address the needs of different communities across the country—especially those that are disadvantaged or feeling left behind. Our elected officials need to hear more from us, their constituents. We can't roll back the climate changes we've already seen. But we can better adapt to and mitigate the risk of warming to us now and for future generations.

The extensive data and case studies throughout this book show a path forward for connecting more people to the issue of climate change and overcoming the three obstacles of polarization, paralysis, and stale/ineffective messaging that stand in the way of solutions. This starts with radically reframing how we think and talk to personalize, individualize, humanize, and localize the climate impacts so they become more relatable to the average person.

We know that 90 percent of Americans are open to constructive climate conversations, as the Global Warming's Six Americas study shows. But no more polar bears, melting icebergs, or world-on-fire imagery. No more doomism. No more calls to save the planet. And maybe the words "climate change" don't always need to be injected into every conversation, at least at first. We can start in different places for different audiences. We can meet people where they are and build bridges to better messengers and validators if needed. If we can rebuild the connective tissue between us, we restore our sense of community. We can bust the myths that hold our movement back, stop the blame and shame game, come together, and stay focused on the solutions that will make a real difference.

We can do this. We know why some movements succeed and why some fail. We know how the most effective campaigns are won. Even as things change, fundamental human truths remain steady.

We know there is a growing new climate denialism based on the system being too hard to change and fear over rising energy costs. But it will cost us much less to become sustainable than not to. To strengthen our energy independence and energy security, we can redirect funds away from the inherently limited system of fossil fuels to create a system right here at home that harnesses the unlimited power of the sun, wind, waves, geothermal heat, and nuclear energy. We need strong governmental policy actions to reduce greenhouse gas emissions and build resilience in our communities.

These changes won't happen overnight. Much work is needed by us just to build the lens through which we can increase political support for the policies we need to incentivize change. But I am an optimist. To be anything less would be selfish and betray the many years of life I still have left. I believe the United States is exceptional and can lead us out of this challenge, just as we helped to create it. I look forward to the incredible, sustainable future we will build—still with many luxuries but in better harmony within the natural world. Able to adapt to a forever-warmed world and pulled back from the brink. Humanity implementing a longer-term, generational planning mentality. Secure in knowing our story will continue for hundreds or even thousands of years longer.

While we have so far in our history had a legacy of natural destruction, I nevertheless believe humans are just as important as any other species that has ever lived on Earth. The writer and philosopher Alan Watts once said, "Through our eyes, the universe is perceiving itself. Through our ears, the universe is listening to its harmonies. We are the witnesses through which the universe becomes conscious of its glory, of its magnificence."[9]

This sentiment was shared by the astronomer Carl Sagan, who said, "We are a way for the universe to know itself."[10]

Humanity is the only species on Earth that can even attempt to understand and appreciate the beauty and scale of the universe. We can find purpose in that; a drive to ensure our long-term sustainability and achieve a destiny that seems to have been reserved only for us in all of evolution.

The choices we all make in the next few decades, in the next few years, will determine our future. You have the power to help, even if you aren't comfortable with or interested in politics or policymaking. If you have gained a new personal connection to the warming world around you, if you feel more optimistic and empowered, if you've learned some tools for how to communicate more effectively—even to those you may not agree with on everything—and if you are actively voting and engaging locally, this book's mission will be a success and we will be on a better path to solving climate change.

If you take these steps and radically reframe the issue of climate change for yourself and those around you, your work can help us unite against the biggest threat to our survival we have ever faced. And I can promise you that this *is* something the Earth *will* care about—and will show us. Because if we do these things, the Earth will allow us to continue to live here.

NOTES

Author's Note

1. PBS NewsHour, "Utility Assistance Frozen after Trump Administration Fires Program's Staff," *PBS NewsHour*, April 24, 2025. https://www.pbs.org/newshour/show/utility-assistance-frozen-after-trump-administration-fires-programs-staff.

Introduction

1. Bella Maharaj, "CIRCLE Releases Preliminary Findings about Youth Voting Patterns in 2024 Election," *The Tufts Daily*, November 5, 2024, https://www.tuftsdaily.com/article/2024/11/circle-releases-preliminary-findings-about-youth-voting-patterns-in-2024-election.

2. "A Comprehensive New Data Analysis: Why Harris Lost in 2024," *Cook Political Report*, May 19, 2025, https://www.cookpolitical.com/analysis/national/national-politics/comprehensive-new-data-analysis-why-harris-lost-2024.

3. Elena Moore, "Unpacking the 2024 Youth Vote: Here's What We Know so Far," *NPR*, November 7, 2024, https://www.npr.org/2024/11/07/g-s1-33331/unpacking-the-2024-youth-vote-heres-what-we-know-so-far.

4. Megan Brenan, "Economy Remains Most Important Issue for 2024 Presidential Vote," *Gallup*, March 28, 2024, https://news.gallup.com/poll/651719/economy-important-issue-2024-presidential-vote.aspx.

5. Environmental Voter Project, "Exit Poll: Climate Voters Were Harris's Strongest Supporters," November 15, 2024, https://environmentalvoter.org/updates/exit-poll-climate-voters-were-harriss-strongest-supporters.

6. Simon Evans and Verner Viisainen, "Analysis: Trump Election Win Could Add 4bn Tonnes to US Emissions by 2030," *Carbon Brief*, March 6, 2024,

https://www.carbonbrief.org/analysis-trump-election-win-could-add-4bn-tonnes-to-us-emissions-by-2030/.

7 Mark Trumbull, "Trump vs. Biden: A Voter Choice on Energy and Climate," *The Christian Science Monitor*, November 8, 2024, https://www.csmonitor.com/Environment/2024/1108/energy-climate-oil-renewables-trump.

8 John Holbein and D. Sunshine Hillygus, "Making Young Voters: The Impact of Preregistration on Youth Turnout," *SSRN Scholarly Paper*, July 16, 2021, https://papers.ssrn.com/sol3/papers.cfm?abstract_id=3918955.

Chapter 1

1 Georgetown University Institute of Politics and Public Service, "New Poll: 81% of Voters Believe Democracy Is Threatened," *GU Politics*, March 21, 2024, https://politics.georgetown.edu/2024/03/21/new-poll-81-of-voters-believe-democracy-is-threatened/.

2 Pew Research Center, "Americans Take a Dim View of the Nation's Future, Look More Positively at the Past," *Pew Research Center*, April 24, 2023, https://www.pewresearch.org/short-reads/2023/04/24/americans-take-a-dim-view-of-the-nations-future-look-more-positively-at-the-past/.

3 American Psychiatric Association, "More Americans Say Climate Change Is Having an Impact on Mental Health Now Than in 2022, APA Survey Finds," *APA Newsroom*, June 18, 2024, https://www.psychiatry.org/News-room/News-Releases/More-Americans-Say-Climate-Change-Is-Having-an-Imp.

4 American Psychiatric Association, "Climate Change and Mental Health: New APA Poll Shows Growing Awareness, Anxiety," *American Psychiatric Association*, October 20, 2020, https://www.psychiatry.org/news-room/news-releases/climate-poll-2020.

5 Ayana Elizabeth Johnson, *What If We Get It Right?: Visions of Climate Futures* (New York: One World, 2023), 3–4.

6 U.S. Energy Information Administration, "Electricity in the U.S.: Generation, Capacity, and Sales," *EIA*, accessed November 1, 2023, https://www.eia.gov/energyexplained/electricity/electricity-in-the-us-generation-capacity-and-sales.php.

7. Reuters, "EIA Sees 23% of US Coal-Generated Power Capacity Retired by End-2029," *Reuters*, November 7, 2022, https://www.reuters.com/business/energy/eia-sees-23-us-coal-generated-power-capacity-retired-by-end-2029-2022-11-07/.

8. International Energy Agency, *Renewables 2024: Executive Summary* (Paris: IEA, 2024), https://www.iea.org/reports/renewables-2024/executive-summary.

9. "Senate's Big, Beautiful Bill Would Be a Disaster for Clean Energy," *Canary Media*, July 10, 2024, https://www.canarymedia.com/articles/policy-regulation/senates-big-beautiful-bill-would-be-a-disaster-for-clean-energy.

10. Dan Gearino, "Inside Clean Energy: Texas Is a Wind and Solar Powerhouse, Despite Lawmakers' Hostility," *Inside Climate News*, March 9, 2023, https://insideclimatenews.org/news/09032023/inside-clean-energy-texas-renewables/.

11. International Energy Agency, "Massive Global Growth of Renewables to 2030 Is Set to Match Entire Power Capacity of Major Economies Today, Moving World Closer to Tripling Goal," *IEA*, January 11, 2024, https://www.iea.org/news/massive-global-growth-of-renewables-to-2030-is-set-to-match-entire-power-capacity-of-major-economies-today-moving-world-closer-to-tripling-goal.

12. Our World in Data, "Levelized Cost of Energy," accessed April 12, 2025, https://ourworldindata.org/grapher/levelized-cost-of-energy.

13. We Are Still In and America's Pledge, *Talanoa Dialogue Submission*, April 2, 2018, United Nations Framework Convention on Climate Change, https://unfccc.int/sites/default/files/resource/212_We%20Are%20Still%20In%20and%20Americas%20Pledge_Talanoa%20Dialogue%20submission_2%20April%202018.pdf.

14. Will Hackman, "The Rise of Cities and States in Fighting Climate Change," *Medium*, August 28, 2019, https://willhackman.medium.com/the-rise-of-cities-and-states-in-fighting-climate-change-6a307bebffb1.

15. Hannah Ritchie, *Not the End of the World: How We Can Be the First Generation to Build a Sustainable Planet* (New York: Little, Brown Spark, 2024), 9.

16. Breakthrough—National Centre for Climate Restoration, *What Lies Beneath: The Understatement of Existential Climate Risk*, 2018, https://www.breakthroughonline.org.au/_files/ugd/148cb0_085aaeb2f1a1481789014b8e895ad23b.pdf.

Chapter 2

1. Mark Trumbull, "Trump vs. Biden: A Voter Choice on Energy and Climate," *The Christian Science Monitor*, November 8, 2024, https://www.csmonitor.com/Environment/2024/1108/energy-climate-oil-renewables-trump.

2. International Renewable Energy Agency (IRENA), *Renewable Power Generation Costs in 2023* (Abu Dhabi: IRENA, September 2024), https://www.irena.org/-/media/Files/IRENA/Agency/Publication/2024/Sep/IRENA_Renewable_power_generation_costs_in_2023.pdf.

3. U.S. Energy Information Administration, "EIA Projects Global Electricity Demand Will Increase Through 2050, Led by Growth in Asia," *EIA*, February 7, 2024, https://www.eia.gov/pressroom/releases/press542.php; International Energy Agency, *World Energy Outlook 2022: Key Findings* (Paris: IEA, 2022), https://www.iea.org/reports/world-energy-outlook-2022/key-findings.

4. U.S. Energy Information Administration, "EIA Projects Global Electricity Demand Will Increase Through 2050, Led by Growth in Asia."

5. Jessica Jewell, Aleh Cherp, and Keywan Riahi, "Energy Transitions and the Divergence of Capacity and Generation in Climate Mitigation Scenarios," *Energy Strategy Reviews* 26 (November 2019): 100409, https://www.sciencedirect.com/science/article/abs/pii/S2214629618312246.

6. American Petroleum Institute, "About That 'Peak Oil Demand,'" *API Blog*, June 21, 2023, https://www.api.org/news-policy-and-issues/blog/2023/06/21/about-peak-oil-demand.

7. Friends of the Earth, "Permitting Reform: Real Solutions, Not More Fossil Fuels," *Friends of the Earth*, accessed April 12, 2025, https://foe.org/permitting-reform-real-solutions-fossil-fuels/.

8. World Economic Forum, "Renewables Are the World's Cheapest Source of Energy," *World Economic Forum*, July 2021, https://www.weforum.org/stories/2021/07/renewables-cheapest-energy-source/; Reuters, "Record Renewables Growth Fuels Cost Competitiveness, IRENA Report Shows," *Reuters*, September 24, 2024, https://www.reuters.com/business/energy/record-renewables-growth-fuels-cost-competitiveness-irena-report-shows-2024-09-24/; United Nations, "Renewable Energy," *United Nations*, accessed July 11, 2025, https://www.un.org/en/climatechange/raising-ambition/renewable-energy/.

9 U.S. Energy Information Administration, "How Much of U.S. Carbon Dioxide Emissions Are Associated with Electricity Generation?" *EIA*, accessed November 16, 2023, https://www.eia.gov/tools/faqs/faq.php?id=709&t=6.

10 U.S. Energy Information Administration, *U.S. Oil and Natural Gas Wells by Production Rate* (Washington, DC: U.S. Department of Energy, December 2024), https://www.eia.gov/petroleum/wells/; U.S. Department of Transportation, Pipeline and Hazardous Materials Safety Administration, "General Pipeline FAQs," *PHMSA*, accessed April 12, 2025, https://www.phmsa.dot.gov/faqs/general-pipeline-faqs.

11 U.S. Energy Information Administration, "Most U.S. Coal Is Used in the Electric Power Sector," *Today in Energy*, February 26, 2024, https://www.eia.gov/todayinenergy/detail.php?id=61545.

12 Priscila Barrera, "Top 10 Natural Gas-Producing Countries (Updated 2023)," *Investing News Network*, August 17, 2023, https://investingnews.com/top-natural-gas-producers/.

13 The New York Times, "How China Became the World's Clean Energy Superpower," *The New York Times*, June 30, 2025, https://www.nytimes.com/interactive/2025/06/30/climate/china-clean-energy-power.html.

14 Interstate Renewable Energy Council (IREC), "National Solar Jobs Census 2023," *IREC*, accessed April 12, 2025, https://irecusa.org/programs/solar-jobs-census/#:~:text=Jobs%20Census%202023-,National%20Solar%20Jobs%20Census%023,annual%20National%20Solar%20Jobs%20Census; Julian Spector, "Chart: Which States Have the Most Solar and Wind Power Jobs?" *Canary Media*, August 23, 2023, https://www.canarymedia.com/articles/clean-energy-jobs/chart-which-states-have-the-most-solar-and-wind-power-jobs.

15 The White House, "Temporary Withdrawal of All Areas on the Outer Continental Shelf from Offshore Wind Leasing and Review of the Federal Government's Leasing and Permitting Practices for Wind Projects," *The White House*, January 2025, https://www.whitehouse.gov/presidential-actions/2025/01/temporary-withdrawal-of-all-areas-on-the-outer-continental-shelf-from-offshore-wind-leasing-and-review-of-the-federal-governments-leasing-and-permitting-practices-for-wind-projects/.

16 Oceana, "Offshore Wind by the Numbers: State-by-State Analysis," *Oceana USA*, accessed April 12, 2025, https://usa.oceana.org/offshore-wind-state-state-analysis/#:~:text=Virginia%3A%20Virginia%20could%20meet%20at,nearly%20%241.9%20billion%20each%20year.

17 Oceana, "Offshore Wind Report: Key Findings," *Oceana USA*, accessed April 12, 2025, https://usa.oceana.org/offshore-wind-report-key-findings/.

18 U.S. Department of the Interior, *Secretary Order 3415: Temporary Suspension of Delegated Authority*, January 2025, https://www.doi.gov//document-library/secretary-order/3415-temporary-suspension-delegated-authority.

19 Lisa Friedman, "Trump Declares Climate National Emergency to Expand Fossil Fuel Development," *The New York Times*, January 22, 2025, https://www.nytimes.com/2025/01/22/climate/trump-national-emergencies.html.

20 Statista, "Resident Population of the United States from 2022 to 2050," *Statista*, accessed July 11, 2025, https://www.statista.com/statistics/183481/united-states-population-projection/.

21 Reuters, "US Power Use to Reach Record Highs in 2025 and 2026, EIA Says," *Reuters*, July 8, 2025, https://www.reuters.com/business/energy/us-power-use-reach-record-highs-2025-2026-eia-says-2025-07-08/.

22 Power Engineering, "One 'Big, Beautiful' Bill Signed into Law Reflects De-prioritization of Renewable Energy," *Power Engineering*, July 9, 2025, https://www.power-eng.com/business/policy-and-regulation/one-big-beautiful-bill-signed-into-law-reflects-de-prioritization-of-renewable-energy/.

23 United States Government, *United States Mid-Century Strategy for Deep Decarbonization*, November 2016, https://unfccc.int/sites/default/files/mid_century_strategy_report-final_red.pdf.

24 U.S. Department of Energy, "DOE Report Shows Clean Energy Jobs Grew More than Twice the Rate of Overall U.S.U.S. Employment," *Department of Energy*, June 28, 2023, https://www.energy.gov/articles/doe-report-shows-clean-energy-jobs-grew-more-twice-rate-overall-us-employment.

25 U.S. Energy Information Administration, "How Much Carbon Dioxide Is Produced per Kilowatthour of U.S. Electricity Generation?" *EIA*, accessed February 2, 2023, https://www.eia.gov/tools/faqs/faq.php?id=727&t=6.

26 The White House, "Reinvigorating America's Beautiful Clean Coal Industry and Amending Executive Order 14241," *The White House*, April 2025, https://www.whitehouse.gov/presidential-actions/2025/04/reinvigorating-americas-beautiful-clean-coal-industry-and-amending-executive-order-14241/.

27 University College London, "Fossil Fuel Air Pollution Responsible for 1 in 5 Deaths Worldwide," *UCL News*, February 9, 2021, https://www.ucl.ac.uk/news/2021/feb/fossil-fuel-air-pollution-responsible-1-5-deaths-worldwide.

28 Harvard T.H. Chan School of Public Health, "Particulate Pollution from Coal Associated with Double the Risk of Mortality Than PM2.5 from Other Sources," *Harvard T.H. Chan School of Public Health News*, June 13, 2022, https://hsph.harvard.edu/news/particulate-pollution-from-coal-associated-with-double-the-risk-of-mortality-than-pm2-5-from-other-sources/.

29 Institute for Energy Economics and Financial Analysis (IEEFA), "U.S. on Track to Close Half of Its Coal Capacity by 2026," *IEEFA*, October 4, 2023, https://ieefa.org/resources/us-track-close-half-coal-capacity-2026.

30 Ben Levitan, "Mercury Pollution from Coal Plants Is Still a Danger to Americans—We Need Stronger Standards to Protect Us," *EDF Climate 411*, February 22, 2022, https://blogs.edf.org/climate411/2022/02/22/mercury-pollution-from-coal-plants-is-still-a-danger-to-americans-we-need-stronger-standards-to-protect-us/.

31 Thomas Cmar, "New Wastewater Treatment Standards for Coal-Fired Power Plants," *Earthjustice*, July 31, 2023, https://earthjustice.org/experts/thomas-cmar/new-wastewater-treatment-standards-for-coal-fired-power-plants.

32 U.S. Environmental Protection Agency, "EPA Announces It Will Reconsider 2024 Water Pollution Limits for Coal Power Plants to Help Protect Communities," *EPA*, February 15, 2023, https://www.epa.gov/newsreleases/epa-announces-it-will-reconsider-2024-water-pollution-limits-coal-power-plants-help.

33 U.S. Energy Information Administration, "Electricity in the U.S.," *EIA*, accessed March 8, 2024, https://www.eia.gov/energyexplained/electricity/electricity-in-the-us.php.

34 World Nuclear Association, "Carbon Dioxide Emissions from Electricity," *World Nuclear Association*, accessed April 12, 2025, https://world-nuclear.org/information-library/energy-and-the-environment/carbon-dioxide-emissions-from-electricity.

35 U.S. Geological Survey, "Which Country Has the Most Coal?" *USGS*, accessed April 12, 2025, https://www.usgs.gov/faqs/which-country-has-most-coal.

36 Worldometer, "U.S. Coal," *Worldometer*, accessed April 12, 2025, https://www.worldometers.info/coal/us-coal/.

37 Statista, "U.S. Petroleum Imports from OPEC Countries 2000–2022," *Statista*, accessed April 12, 2025, https://www.statista.com/statistics/190966/petroleum-imports-into-the-us-from-opec-countries-since-2000/.

38 U.S. Energy Information Administration, "How Much Carbon Dioxide Is Produced per Kilowatthour of U.S. Electricity Generation?"

39 U.S. Energy Information Administration, "Where Our Natural Gas Comes From," *EIA*, accessed July 20, 2023, https://www.eia.gov/energyexplained/natural-gas/where-our-natural-gas-comes-from.php; U.S. Energy Information Administration, *Natural Gas Annual*, accessed April 12, 2025, https://www.eia.gov/naturalgas/annual/#:~:text=Total%20imports%20of%20natural%20gas,for%20the%20ninth%20consecutive%20year.

40 U.S. Energy Information Administration, "U.S. Coal Imports and Exports," *EIA*, accessed October 3, 2023, https://www.eia.gov/energyexplained/coal/imports-and-exports.php.

41 Jeremy Symons, *Exporting Carbon*, Politico, September 2023, https://www.energy.gov/sites/default/files/2024-06/112.%20Jeremy%20Symons%2C%20Exporting%20Carbon%2C%20Politico%20%28Sept.%023%29.pdf; McKinsey & Company, "Decarbonising India: Charting a Pathway for Sustainable Growth," *McKinsey & Company*, February 20, 2023, https://www.mckinsey.com/capabilities/sustainability/our-insights/decarbonising-india-charting-a-pathway-for-sustainable-growth.

42 Jeremy Symons, "New Study Finds Rising Exports of Oil and Gas Undermines U.S. Action to Reduce Emissions," *Symons Public Affairs*, April 3, 2024, https://www.symonspa.com/post/new-study-finds-rising-exports-of-oil-and-gas-undermines-u-s-action-to-reduce-emissions.

43 Gavin Maguire, "U.S. LNG Export Dominance Tested as Europe's Demand Wilts," *Reuters*, September 4, 2024, https://www.reuters.com/markets/commodities/us-lng-export-dominance-tested-europes-demand-wilts-maguire-2024-09-04/.

44 International Renewable Energy Agency (IRENA), "Fast-Track Energy Transitions to Win the Race to Zero," *IRENA*, March 16, 2021, https://www.irena.org/news/pressreleases/2021/mar/fast-track-energy-transitions--to-win-the-race-to-zero.

45 United Nations, "Renewable Energy," *United Nations Climate Action*, accessed April 12, 2025, https://www.un.org/en/climatechange/raising-ambition/renewable-energy.

46 Riham Alkousaa, "Climate Change Damage Could Cost $38 Trillion per Year by 2050, Study Finds," *Reuters*, April 17, 2024, https://www.reuters.com/business/environment/climate-change-damage-could-cost-38-trillion-per-year-by-2050-study-finds-2024-04-17/.

47 United Nations, "Renewable Energy," *United Nations Climate Action*.

Chapter 3

1. Hannah Ritchie, "Climate Change: Do People Support Policies to Reduce Emissions?" *Our World in Data*, accessed April 12, 2025, https://ourworldindata.org/climate-change-support.

2. United Nations Development Programme, "The World's Largest Survey on Climate Change Is Out. Here's What the Results Show," *UNDP Climate Promise*, January 27, 2021, https://climatepromise.undp.org/news-and-stories/worlds-largest-survey-climate-change-out-heres-what-results-show.

3. Yale Program on Climate Change Communication, *Climate Change in the American Mind: Beliefs & Attitudes—Spring 2024*, Yale University and George Mason University, April 2024, https://climatecommunication.yale.edu/publications/climate-change-in-the-american-mind-beliefs-attitudes-spring-2024/toc/2/.

4. Cary Funk and Alec Tyson, "What the Data Says about Americans' Views of Climate Change," *Pew Research Center*, August 9, 2023, https://www.pewresearch.org/short-reads/2023/08/09/what-the-data-says-about-americans-views-of-climate-change/.

5. Funk and Tyson, "What the Data Says about Americans' Views of Climate Change."

6. Cary Funk, "Americans See Broad Impacts from Climate Change—Including on Their Community," *Pew Research Center*, May 26, 2021, https://www.pewresearch.org/science/2021/05/26/local-impact-of-climate-change-environmental-problems/.

7. Funk and Tyson, "What the Data Says about Americans' Views of Climate Change."

8. Steve Matthews, "IMF Says Public Support Needed to Change Climate Policies," *Bloomberg*, February 10, 2023, https://www.bloomberg.com/news/articles/2023-02-10/imf-says-public-support-needed-to-change-climate-policies.

9. Sarah Kaplan and Andrew Ba Tran, "Hurricane Ida Is the Latest Climate Disaster Showing the Challenge of Adapting," *The Washington Post*, September 4, 2021, https://www.washingtonpost.com/climate-environment/2021/09/04/climate-disaster-hurricane-ida/.

10. Barbara Spindel, "A Naturalist Figured Out Climate Change in 1799. The World Forgot Him," *The Christian Science Monitor*, July 19, 2019, https://

www.csmonitor.com/Books/2019/0719/A-naturalist-figured-out-climate-change-in-1799.-The-world-forgot-him.

11 Andrea Wulf, "Alexander von Humboldt's Warning to the World," *Los Angeles Times*, July 5, 2015, https://www.latimes.com/opinion/op-ed/la-oe-wulf-rediscovering-alexander-von-humboldt-20150705-story.html.

Chapter 4

1 ClimateTrade, "The Evolution of Carbon Footprint Measurement," *ClimateTrade*, March 1, 2023, https://climatetrade.com/the-evolution-of-carbon-footprint-measurement/; Rebecca Solnit, "Big Oil Coined 'Carbon Footprints' to Blame Us for Their Greed. Keep Them on the Hook," *The Guardian*, August 23, 2021, https://www.theguardian.com/commentisfree/2021/aug/23/big-oil-coined-carbon-footprints-to-blame-us-for-their-greed-keep-them-on-the-hook; Our Changing Climate, "The Carbon Footprint Sham," YouTube video, 12:32, April 18, 2023, https://www.youtube.com/watch?v=ywrZPypqSB4.

2 Center for International Environmental Law (CIEL), "BP Acknowledged Climate Risk of Fossil Fuels in 1990," *CIEL*, April 16, 2024, https://www.ciel.org/news/bp-acknowledged-climate-risk-of-fossil-fuels-in-1990/.

3 Andrew Freedman, "Taylor Swift's Jet Emissions and the Climate Blame Game," *Axios*, August 4, 2022, https://www.axios.com/2022/08/04/taylor-swift-private-jet-climate-change.

4 Oxfam International, *Instagram*, accessed April 12, 2025, https://www.instagram.com/oxfaminternational?hl=en.

5 Global Business Travel Association (GBTA), "U.S. Business Travel Industry Responsible for 2% of U.S. GDP and 3.5% of Employment in Latest Full-Year Figures," *GBTA*, July 13, 2023, https://www.gbta.org/u-s-business-travel-industry-responsible-for-2-of-u-s-gdp-and-3-5-of-employment-in-latest-full-year-figures/; U.S. Department of Transportation, Bureau of Transportation Statistics, *America on the Go: Business Travel*, accessed April 12, 2025, https://www.bts.gov/archive/publications/america_on_the_go/us_business_travel/entire.

6 Aradhna E. Tripati et al., "Climate Change Increases Cross-Cultural Sentiment toward Climate Science and Action," *PLOS Climate* 2, no. 6 (June 2023): e0000152, https://pmc.ncbi.nlm.nih.gov/articles/PMC10281825/#fig 1.

7   United Nations Framework Convention on Climate Change (UNFCCC), *The Paris Agreement*, December 2015, https://unfccc.int/sites/default/files/english_paris_agreement.pdf.

8   World Meteorological Organization (WMO), "WMO Confirms 2024 as Warmest Year on Record—About 1.5°C Above Pre-Industrial Level," *WMO*, January 12, 2025, https://wmo.int/news/media-centre/wmo-confirms-2024-warmest-year-record-about-155degc-above-pre-industrial-level.

9   Natalia Liubchenkova, "Every Tenth of a Degree Matters: UN Climate Report Is a Call for Action, Not Despair," *France 24*, March 22, 2023, https://www.france24.com/en/environment/20230322-every-tenth-of-a-degree-matters-un-climate-report-is-a-call-for-action-not-despair.

10 Tripati et al., "Climate Change Increases Cross-Cultural Sentiment toward Climate Science and Action," https://journals.plos.org/climate/article?id=10.1371/journal.pclm.0000152.

Interlude

1   House Select Committee on the Climate Crisis, *Solving the Climate Crisis: The Congressional Action Plan for a Clean Energy Economy and a Healthy, Resilient, and Just America*, US House of Representatives, June 2020, https://castor.house.gov/climatecrisis/sites/climatecrisis.house.gov/files/climate%20crisis%20action%20plan.pdf.

2   David Roberts, "House Democrats' New Climate Plan Is the Most Detailed Ever in the US," *Vox*, June 30, 2020, https://www.vox.com/energy-and-environment/2020/6/30/21305891/aoc-climate-change-house-democrats-select-committee-report.

Chapter 5

1   United Nations Framework Convention on Climate Change (UNFCCC), *Fact Sheet: Climate Change Mitigation*, 2015, https://unfccc.int/files/press/backgrounders/application/pdf/press_factsh_mitigation.pdf.

2   United Nations Framework Convention on Climate Change (UNFCCC), "Introduction to Adaptation and Resilience," *UNFCCC*, accessed April 12, 2025, https://unfccc.int/topics/adaptation-and-resilience/the-big-picture/introduction.

3   United Nations, "Renewable Energy," *United Nations Climate Action*, accessed April 12, 2025, https://www.un.org/en/climatechange/raising-ambition/renewable-energy.

4   National Institute of Building Sciences, *Natural Hazard Mitigation Saves: 2019 Report*, 2019, https://www.nibs.org/files/pdfs/NIBS_MMC_MitigationSaves_2019.pdf.

5   U.S. Chamber of Commerce, *The Preparedness Payoff: The Economic Benefits of Investing in Climate Resilience*, September 7, 2022, https://www.uschamber.com/security/the-preparedness-payoff-the-economic-benefits-of-investing-in-climate-resilience.

6   Intergovernmental Panel on Climate Change (IPCC), "About the IPCC," *IPCC*, accessed April 13, 2025, https://www.ipcc.ch/about/.

7   Intergovernmental Panel on Climate Change (IPCC), *Fact Sheet: Human Settlements—Climate Change 2022: Impacts, Adaptation and Vulnerability*, 2022, https://www.ipcc.ch/report/ar6/wg2/downloads/outreach/IPCC_AR6_WGII_FactSheet_HumanSettlements.pdf.

8   Kate Marvel et al., "Twentieth-Century Hydroclimate Changes Consistent with Human Influence," *Nature* 570 (2019): 344–50, https://www.nature.com/articles/s41586-018-0787-6; ason Samenow, "Raging River and High Tide Coincide to Flood Alexandria, Arlington and the District," *The Washington Post*, June 5, 2018, https://www.washingtonpost.com/news/capital-weather-gang/wp/2018/06/05/raging-river-and-high-tide-coincide-to-flood-alexandria-arlington-and-the-district/.

9   District of Columbia Department of Energy and Environment (DOEE), "Floodplain Mapping," *DOEE*, accessed April 12, 2025, https://doee.dc.gov/floodplainmap.

10 National Mall Underground, "The Problem," *National Mall Underground*, accessed April 12, 2025, https://www.nationalmallunderground.org/problem/; Andrew Beaujon, "17th Street Will Close Tuesday for the Annual Test of a Levee You May Not Know About," *Washingtonian*, October 2, 2020, https://www.washingtonian.com/2020/10/02/17th-street-will-close-tuesday-for-the-annual-test-of-a-levee-you-may-not-know-about/; Scott MacFarlane, "The Flooding Triangle: Some of DC's Iconic Buildings at

Risk in 100-Year Flood," *NBC Washington*, April 30, 2019, https://www.nbcwashington.com/news/local/the-flooding-triangle-some-of-dcs-iconic-buildings-at-risk-in-100-year-flood/113893/.

11 Chelsea Coffin, "Urban Heat Islands: A Rising Threat to the Health of D.C. Residents," *D.C. Policy Center*, August 2, 2021, https://www.dcpolicycenter.org/publications/urban-heat-islands/.

12 Lei Zhao et al., "Residential Cooling Demand and the Implications of Urban Heat for Climate Change Mitigation and Adaptation," *Proceedings of the National Academy of Sciences* 118, no. 23 (June 2021): e2024792118, https://www.pnas.org/doi/10.1073/pnas.2024792118.

13 U.S. House of Representatives, *Final Report of the Select Committee on the Climate Crisis*, 117th Cong., 2nd sess., House Report 117–662, December 2022, https://www.congress.gov/congressional-report/117th-congress/house-report/662/1.

14 Geoffrey Supran and Naomi Oreskes, "Assessing ExxonMobil's Climate Change Communications (1977–2014)," *Nature Climate Change* 9 (2019): 158–63, https://www.nature.com/articles/s41558-018-0315-6.

15 The New York Times, "Heat Wave and Blackout Would Send Half of Phoenix to E.R., Study Says," *The New York Times*, May 23, 2023. https://www.nytimes.com/2023/05/23/climate/blackout-heat-wave-danger.html.

16 U.S. Environmental Protection Agency, "Climate Change Indicators: Heat Waves," *EPA*, accessed July 2023, https://www.epa.gov/climate-indicators/climate-change-indicators-heat-waves.

17 National Weather Service, "Hurricane Katrina——August 2005," *National Weather Service Weather Forecast Office Mobile/Pensacola*, accessed April 12, 2025, https://www.weather.gov/mob/katrina.

18 Richard S. J. Tol, "Quantifying the Consensus on Anthropogenic Global Warming in the Literature: A Re-Analysis," *Climatic Change* 122, no. 1–2 (2014): 395–404, https://link.springer.com/article/10.1007/s10584-013-1011-1.

19 David N. Wear and John W. Coulston, *From Sink to Source: Increasing Fire Emissions Offset Gains in Forest Carbon Sequestration*, U.S. Department of Agriculture, Forest Service, Southern Research Station, 2021, https://research.fs.usda.gov/treesearch/67128.

20 Cary Funk and Alec Tyson, "What the Data Says about Americans' Views of Climate Change," *Pew Research Center*, August 9, 2023, https://www

.pewresearch.org/short-reads/2023/08/09/what-the-data-says-about-americans-views-of-climate-change/.

21. U.S. Government Accountability Office, *Climate Resilience: Options to Enhance the Accountability and Impact of Federal Investments*, GAO-24--106937, March 2024, https://www.gao.gov/products/gao 24 106937.

22. U.S. Department of Housing and Urban Development, *Climate Adaptation Plan: Fiscal Year 2024*, October 2023, https://www.sustainability.gov/pdfs/hud-2024-cap.pdf.

23. The Pew Charitable Trusts, *Wildfires: Burning Through State Budgets*, November 2022, https://www.pewtrusts.org/en/research-and-analysis/reports/2022/11/wildfires-burning-through-state-budgets.

24. Paxton Drew, "Why Every State Needs a Chief Resilience Officer," *Environmental Defense Fund—Growing Returns*, July 28, 2023, https://blogs.edf.org/growingreturns/2023/07/28/why-every-state-needs-a-chief-resilience-officer/.

25. The Pew Charitable Trusts, "West Virginia's Experience Can Inform Flood Resilience Efforts in Other Mountain States," *The Pew Charitable Trusts*, October 26, 2023, https://www.pewtrusts.org/en/research-and-analysis/data-visualizations/2023/west-virginias-experience-can-inform-flood-resilience-efforts-in-other-mountain-states.

26. Virginia Department of Conservation and Recreation, "Flood Awareness," *Virginia DCR*, accessed April 12, 2025, https://www.dcr.virginia.gov/dam-safety-and-floodplains/floodawareness.

27. Voss Law Firm, "Acts of God & Flood Insurance Claims: What Is Covered?" *The Voss Law Firm, P.C.*, accessed April 13, 2025, https://www.vosslawfirm.com/library/acts-of-god-flood-insurance-claims-what-is-covered-.cfm.

28. State Resiliency Office of West Virginia, *State Resiliency Office—West Virginia*, accessed April 12, 2025, https://sro.wv.gov/Pages/default.aspx.

Chapter 6

1. Southern Poverty Law Center, *A Violent History: The Ongoing Impact of Far-Right Extremism in America*, accessed April 12, 2025, https://www.splcenter.org/resources/reports/violent-history/.

2   Guttmacher Institute, "State Bans on Abortion Throughout Pregnancy," *Guttmacher Institute*, accessed April 1, 2024, https://www.guttmacher.org/state-policy/explore/state-policies-abortion-bans.

3   Tony Schwartz, *The Responsive Chord*, accessed April 12, 2025, https://tonyschwartz.org/books/responsive-chord/.

4   Frank Luntz, *Words That Work: It's Not What You Say, It's What People Hear* (New York: Hyperion, 2007), 24.

5   Josh Glancy, "Frank Luntz: The Man Who Came Up with 'Climate Change'—and Regrets It," *The Times*, October 28, 2021, https://www.thetimes.com/article/frank-luntz-the-man-who-came-up-with-climate-change-and-regrets-it-6v6pp00pc.

6   Katharine Q. Seelye, "A Call for Softer, Greener Language," *The New York Times*, March 2, 2003, https://www.nytimes.com/2003/03/02/us/a-call-for-softer-greener-language.html.

7   Anthony Adragna, "Frank Luntz Admits He Was Wrong on Climate Change," *Politico*, August 21, 2019, https://www.politico.com/story/2019/08/21/frank-luntz-wrong-climate-change-1470653.

8   National Conference of State Legislatures, "The Role of Forests in Carbon Sequestration and Storage," *NCSL*, accessed April 13, 2025, https://www.ncsl.org/environment-and-natural-resources/the-role-of-forests-in-carbon-sequestration-and-storage.

9   United Nations Framework Convention on Climate Change (UNFCCC), "The Paris Agreement," *UNFCCC*, accessed April 12, 2025, https://unfccc.int/process-and-meetings/the-paris-agreement/the-paris-agreement.

10 The White House, "President Trump Signs One Trillion Trees Executive Order, Promoting Conservation and Regeneration of Nation's Forests," *Trump White House Archives*, October 13, 2020, https://trumpwhitehouse.archives.gov/articles/president-trump-signs-one-trillion-trees-executive-order-promoting-conservation-regeneration-nations-forests/.

11 Jeremy B. C. Jackson et al., "The Magnitude and Impacts of Anthropogenic Global Changes on Nature and Humanity," *Biological Conservation* 253 (2021): 108527, https://www.sciencedirect.com/science/article/pii/S0006320721002767.

12 United States Government, *United States Mid-Century Strategy for Deep Decarbonization*, November 2016, https://unfccc.int/files/focus/long-term_strategies/application/pdf/mid_century_strategy_report-final_red.pdf.

13 United States Government, *United States Mid-Century Strategy for Deep Decarbonization*.

14 U.S. Department of Agriculture, "Biden-Harris Administration Announces Plans for Reforestation, Climate Adaptation, Including New Resources," *USDA*, July 25, 2022, https://www.usda.gov/about-usda/news/press-releases/2022/07/25/biden-harris-administration-announces-plans-reforestation-climate-adaptation-including-new-resources.

15 U.S. Department of Agriculture, *Reforestation Strategy: A Plan for Reforestation on National Forest System Lands*, July 2022, https://www.usda.gov/sites/default/files/documents/reforestation-strategy.pdf.

16 The Wilderness Society, "Federal Lands Emissions Accountability Tool," *The Wilderness Society*, accessed April 13, 2025, https://www.wilderness.org/articles/article/federal-lands-emissions-accountability-tool.

17 United States Government, *United States Mid-Century Strategy for Deep Decarbonization*.

18 United States Government, *United States Mid-Century Strategy for Deep Decarbonization*.

19 Biomass Energy Resource Center, "Grass Energy Basics," *Biomass Energy Resource Center*, accessed April 12, 2025, https://www.biomasscenter.org/resource-library/fact-sheets/grass-energy-basics.

20 A. A. Agboola, D. F. Akinola, and O. J. Akinyemi, "The Microbial Biomass Properties of a Savanna Soil under Improved Grass and Legume Pastures in Northern Nigeria," accessed April 12, 2025, https://www.researchgate.net/publication/257015425_The_microbial_biomass_properties_of_a_savanna_soil_under_improved_grass_and_legume_pastures_in_northern_Nigeria.

21 R. M. Ibbett, L. G. Riley, and N. G. T. Hadders, "Grass as a Feedstock for Bioenergy: Chemical Composition and Comparison with Other Biomass Feedstocks," *Energy Procedia* 128 (2017): 73–80, https://www.sciencedirect.com/science/article/pii/S1876610217319410.

22 Chatham House, "The Growing Role of BECCS," *Chatham House*, January 2020, https://www.chathamhouse.org/2020/01/net-zero-and-beyond-what-role-bioenergy-carbon-capture-and-storage-0/growing-role-beccs.

23 United States Government, *The Long-Term Strategy of the United States: Pathways to Net-Zero Greenhouse Gas Emissions by 2050*, November 2021, https://unfccc.int/sites/default/files/resource/US-LongTermStrategy-2021.pdf.

24 The White House. "Fact Sheet: President Donald J. Trump Rapidly Expands Timber Production," March 1, 2025, https://www.whitehouse.gov/fact-sheets/2025/03/fact-sheet-president-donald-j-trump-rapidly-expands-timber-production/.

25 The Pew Charitable Trusts, "Coastal 'Blue Carbon': An Important Tool for Combating Climate Change," *The Pew Charitable Trusts*, September 20, 2021, https://www.pewtrusts.org/en/research-and-analysis/issue-briefs/2021/09/coastal-blue-carbon-an-important-tool-for-combating-climate-change.

26 Congressional Research Service, *Federal Land Ownership: Overview and Data*, R42346, updated February 21, 2020, https://sgp.fas.org/crs/misc/R42346.pdf.

27 Statista, "Total Area of Land in Farms in the United States from 2000 to 2023," *Statista*, accessed April 13, 2025, https://www.statista.com/statistics/196104/total-area-of-land-in-farms-in-the-us-since-2000/.

28 Brookings Institution, "The Future of the Paris Climate Regime," *Brookings*, December 12, 2023, https://www.brookings.edu/on-the-record/the-future-of-the-paris-climate-regime/.

Chapter 7

1 Hannah Ritchie, *Not the End of the World: How We Can Be the First Generation to Build a Sustainable Planet* (New York: Little, Brown Spark, 2024), 6–7.

2 *Carville: Winning Is Everything, Stupid!*, directed by Matt Tyrnauer (New York: Greenwich Entertainment, 2024), documentary film.

3 Michael Scherer and David Weigel, "Democrats Take Three Midwest States That Sealed Trump's Victory," *The Washington Post*, November 7, 2018, https://www.washingtonpost.com/politics/2018/live-updates/midterms/midterm-election-updates/democrats-take-three-midwest-states-that-sealed-trumps-victory/.

4 Michael Shank, "Governor DeSantis's 'Don't Say Climate Change' Law Won't Fly with Voters," *Covering Climate Now*, April 9, 2024, https://coveringclimatenow.org/from-us-story/governor-desantiss-dont-say-climate-change-law-wont-fly-with-voters/.

5 Cook Political Report, "House Race Ratings," *Cook Political Report with Amy Walter*, accessed April 13, 2025, https://www.cookpolitical.com/ratings/house-race-ratings.

6 Cook Political Report, "Senate Race Ratings," *Cook Political Report with Amy Walter*, accessed April 13, 2025, https://www.cookpolitical.com/ratings/senate-race-ratings.

7 Emily Badger and Kevin Quealy, "Why Having the Governor's Mansion Doesn't Mean You Can Actually Govern," *The New York Times*, November 12, 2021, https://www.nytimes.com/2021/11/12/us/politics/democrats-trifecta-power.html.

8 Turning Point USA, "Meet the Founder," *TPUSA*, accessed April 13, 2025, https://www.tpusa.com/meetthefounder.

9 Charlie Kirk, "This Is the Most Important Election of Our Lifetime," YouTube video, 10:41, March 19, 2024, https://www.youtube.com/watch?v=NcUAg2eRRw4.

10 Yale Program on Climate Change Communication, "Global Warming's Six Americas," *Yale University*, accessed April 13, 2025, https://climatecommunication.yale.edu/about/projects/global-warmings-six-americas/.

11 Yale Program on Climate Change Communication, "Global Warming's Six Americas."

12 Katharine Hayhoe, *Saving Us: A Climate Scientist's Case for Hope and Healing in a Divided World* (New York: Atria/One Signal Publishers, 2021), 9–10.

13 Potential Energy Coalition, "Global Report," *Potential Energy Coalition*, accessed April 13, 2025, https://potentialenergycoalition.org/guides-and-reports/global-report/.

Chapter 8

1 Pew Research Center, "How Closely Are Americans Following Election News, and What Are They Seeing?" October 10, 2024. https://www.pewresearch.org/journalism/2024/10/10/how-closely-are-americans-following-election-news-and-what-are-they-seeing/.

2   Megan Brenan, "Attention to Political News Slips Back to Typical Levels," *Gallup*, January 18, 2024, https://news.gallup.com/poll/513128/attention-political-news-slips-back-typical-levels.aspx.

3   Ezra Klein, "Yanna Krupnikov on Why Americans Tune Out Politics," *The New York Times*, June 18, 2024, https://www.nytimes.com/2024/06/18/opinion/ezra-klein-podcast-yanna-krupnikov.html.

4   Sydney Hartman, "Who Are Low-Propensity Voters and How Are the Trump and Harris Campaigns Targeting Them?" *WVTM 13*, October 28, 2024, https://www.wvtm13.com/article/who-are-low-propensity-voters-election/62736805.

5   Claire Hansen, "How Many People Didn't Vote in the 2024 Election?" *U.S.News & World Report*, November 15, 2024, https://www.usnews.com/news/national-news/articles/2024-11-15/how-many-people-didnt-vote-in-the-2024-election.

6   Alexander Nazaryan, "Andrew Breitbart Was Right: Politics Is Downstream from Culture," *Newsweek*, March 28, 2024, https://www.newsweek.com/andrew-breitbart-mark-zuckerberg-two-way-politics-culture-street-opinion-2012865.

7   "The Mind Body Ecology Institute," accessed May 15, 2025, https://www.mindbodyecologyinstitute.org.

Chapter 9

1   Alejandra Borunda, "Cities Are Stepping Up to Cut Emissions, but They Can't Do It Alone," *National Geographic*, March 19, 2019, https://www.nationalgeographic.com/science/article/city-consumption-greenhouse-gases-carbon-c40-spd.

2   Devashree Saha and Mark Muro, "Pledges and Progress: Steps Toward Greenhouse Gas Emissions Reductions in the 100 Largest Cities across the United States," *Brookings Institution*, December 13, 2016, https://www.brookings.edu/research/pledges-and-progress-steps-toward-greenhouse-gas-emissions-reductions-in-the-100-largest-cities-across-the-united-states/.

3   Emma Johnson, "Are U.S. Cities Reducing Greenhouse Gas Emissions at an Adequate Pace?" *American Council for an Energy-Efficient Economy*

(ACEEE), June 29, 2022, https://www.aceee.org/blog-post/2022/06/are-us-cities-reducing-greenhouse-gas-emissions-adequate-pace.

4. FOX 55 DC Staff, "Virginia Parents Protest Critical Race Theory Outside Loudoun County School Board Meeting," *FOX DC*, June 23, 2021, https://www.fox5dc.com/news/virginia-parents-protest-critical-race-theory-outside-loudoun-county-school-board-meeting.

5. Fight for Schools, "Fight for Schools Launches Ads in Two Congressional Races (VA-10 and VA-07)," *Fight for Schools*, April 1, 2024, https://fightforschools.com/fight-for-schools-launches-ads-in-two-congressional-races-va-10-and-va-07/.

6. Nick Minock, "Sexual Assaults in Loudoun County Public Schools Outrage Parents, Lead to School Board Ouster," *WJLA*, January 4, 2023, https://wjla.com/news/crisis-in-the-classrooms/sexual-assaults-loudoun-county-public-schools-outraged-loudoun-county-parents-oust-school-board-2023-grand-jury-report-scott-ziegler-wayde-bayard-abbie-platt-ian-prior-fight-for-schools-nick-gothard-loudoun-4-all.

7. Michael Moline, "Moms for Liberty Now Has 310 Chapters in 48 States. What Will They Do Now?" *Florida Phoenix*, February 2, 2024, https://floridaphoenix.com/2024/02/02/moms-for-liberty-now-has-310-chapters-in-48-states-what-will-they-do-now/.

8. Office of Governor Gretchen Whitmer, "Governor Whitmer Signs Historic Clean Energy, Climate Action Package," *Michigan.gov*, November 28, 2023, https://www.michigan.gov/whitmer/news/press-releases/2023/11/28/governor-whitmer-signs-historic-clean-energy-climate-action-package.

9. Clean Energy States Alliance, "100% Clean Energy Collaborative Guide," *CESA*, accessed April 13, 2025, https://www.cesa.org/projects/100-clean-energy-collaborative/guide/.

10. The Climate Reality Project, "Branches," *The Climate Reality Project*, accessed April 13, 2025, https://www.climaterealityproject.org/branches.

11. Citizens' Climate Lobby, *Citizens' Climate Lobby*, accessed April 13, 2025, https://citizensclimatelobby.org/.

12. Flannery Winchester, "Breaking the Climate Silence: How CCLers Held Tens of Thousands of Climate Conversations," *Citizens' Climate Lobby*, January 12, 2024, https://citizensclimatelobby.org/blog/grassroots/breaking-the-climate-silence-how-cclers-held-tens-of-thousands-of-climate-conversations/.

Chapter 10

1. *New York Times*, "Trump's 'DOGE' Cuts: Which U.S. Federal Employees Are Most Likely to Lose Their Jobs?," March 28, 2025, https://www.nytimes.com/interactive/2025/03/28/us/politics/trump-doge-federal-job-cuts.html.

2. Representative Michael Cloud, "GOP Lawmakers Tackle Challenge of Turning Trump Actions into Laws," *U.S. House of Representatives*, February 23, 2025, https://cloud.house.gov/posts/gop-lawmakers-tackle-challenge-of-turning-trump-actions-into-laws.

3. Jerusalem Demsas, "Liberals Can't Blame Trump for California: Derek Thompson and Ezra Klein on their new book, Abundance," *The Atlantic*, March 18, 2025, https://www.theatlantic.com/podcasts/archive/2025/03/derek-thompson-and-ezra-klein-abundance/682077/.

4. U.S. Environmental Protection Agency, "EPA Launches Biggest Deregulatory Action in U.S. History," *EPA*, March 12, 2025, https://www.epa.gov/newsreleases/epa-launches-biggest-deregulatory-action-us-history.

5. Environmental and Energy Study Institute, "Fact Sheet: Proposals to Reduce Fossil Fuel Subsidies," *EESI*, January 2024, https://www.eesi.org/papers/view/fact-sheet-proposals-to-reduce-fossil-fuel-subsidies-january-2024.

6. U.S. Department of State, "Remarks on the Paris Agreement," Secretary John Kerry, November 16, 2016, https://2009-2017.state.gov/secretary/remarks/2016/11/264366.htm.

7. Advanced Research Projects Agency–Energy (ARPA-E), *ARPA-E Strategic Vision Roadmap*, 2022, https://arpa-e.energy.gov/sites/default/files/migrated/2022%20ARPA-E%20Strategic%20Vision%20Roadmap.pdf.

8. Associated Press, "Energy Chief Praises Research Hub That Trump Once Sought to Ax," *Rigzone*, March 18, 2025, https://www.rigzone.com/news/wire/energy_chief_praises_research_hub_that_trump_once_sought_to_ax-18-mar-2025-179960-article/.

9. United Nations Industrial Development Organization (UNIDO), "Steel and Cement Can Drive a Decade of Action on Climate Change—Here's How," *Industrial Analytics Platform*, accessed April 13, 2025, https://iap.unido.org/articles/steel-and-cement-can-drive-decade-action-climate-change-how.

10 World Economic Forum, "Can Cement Production Become More Sustainable?" *World Economic Forum*, September 2024, https://www.weforum.org/stories/2024/09/cement-production-sustainable-concrete-co2-emissions/.

11 Bill Gates, "Lowering Green Premiums," *Gates Notes*, accessed April 13, 2025, https://www.gatesnotes.com/lowering-green-premiums.

12 Bill Gates, *How to Avoid a Climate Disaster: The Solutions We Have and the Breakthroughs We Need* (New York: Alfred A. Knopf, 2021), 108.

13 Sitka Conservation Society, "The Salmon Forest," *Sitka Conservation Society*, accessed April 13, 2025, https://www.sitkawild.org/the_salmon_forest.

14 Justin Catanoso, "End Old-Growth Logging in Carbon-Rich 'Crown Jewel' of U.S. Forests: Study," *Mongabay*, June 1, 2022, https://news.mongabay.com/2022/06/end-old-growth-logging-in-carbon-rich-crown-jewel-of-u-s-forests-study/.

15 Southeast Alaska Conservation Council, "Tongass," *SEACC*, accessed April 13, 2025, https://seacc.org/our-work/tongass/.

16 Virginia Department of Conservation and Recreation, "State Parks Friend Groups," *Virginia DCR*, accessed April 13, 2025, https://www.dcr.virginia.gov/state-parks/friend-groups.

17 National Park Service, "Theodore Roosevelt and Conservation," *U.S. National Park Service*, accessed April 13, 2025, https://www.nps.gov/thro/learn/historyculture/theodore-roosevelt-and-conservation.htm.

18 Papahānaumokuākea Marine National Monument, "History Lecture: Origins of Papahānaumokuākea," *Papahānaumokuākea Marine National Monument*, accessed April 13, 2025, https://www.papahanaumokuakea.gov/tenth/history_lecture.html.

19 John Briley, "President Signs Landmark Law Protecting Wild Lands and Rivers," *The Pew Charitable Trusts*, March 12, 2019, https://www.pewtrusts.org/en/research-and-analysis/articles/2019/03/12/president-signs-landmark-law-protecting-wild-lands-and-rivers.

20 Southern Utah Wilderness Alliance, "Trump's Assault on Utah Monuments Leaves Millions of Acres in Limbo," *SUWA*, December 5, 2017, https://suwa.org/trumps-assault-utah-monuments-leaves-millions-acres-limbo/.

21 The White House, "Executive Order on Unleashing American Energy," *The White House*, January 20, 2025, https://www.whitehouse.gov/presidential-actions/2025/01/unleashing-american-energy/.

22 RNZ News, "Trump's Executive Order to Open Vast Marine Reserve in Pacific Waters to Commercial Fishing Draws Mixed Reactions," *RNZ*, January 22, 2025, https://www.rnz.co.nz/international/pacific-news/558881/trump-s-executive-order-to-open-vast-marine-reserve-in-pacific-waters-to-commercial-fishing-draws-mixed-reactions.

23 National Park Service, "2022 Visitor Spending Contributed $710 Million to Local Economy," *U.S. National Park Service*, August 24, 2023, https://www.nps.gov/grca/learn/news/2022-visitor-spending-to-grand-canyon-national-park.htm.

24 National Park Service, "2022 Visitor Spending Contributed $710 Million to Local Economy."

25 Katie Arnold, "What Sally Jewell's Nomination Means for the Outdoor Industry," *Outside*, February 6, 2013, https://www.outsideonline.com/outdoor-adventure/environment/what-sally-jewells-nomination-means-outdoor-industry/.

26 Outdoor Industry Association, *The Outdoor Recreation Economy*, April 2017, https://outdoorindustry.org/wp-content/uploads/2017/04/OIA_RecEconomy_FINAL_Single.pdf.

27 Alaska Cruise Association, "Alaska Cruise History," *Alaska Cruise Association*, accessed April 13, 2025, https://akcruise.org/economy/alaska-cruise-history/.

28 Alex Bridges, "Tourism Expert Encourages Front Royal to Lean into Its Identity," *The Northern Virginia Daily*, March 13, 2024, https://www.nvdaily.com/nvdaily/tourism-expert-encourages-front-royal-to-lean-into-its-identity/article_f8cbb0d7-a93f-5b4d-9506-20655ff74f38.html.

29 BBC News, "Cuts to National Parks and Forests Met with Backlash," *BBC News*, March 1, 2025, https://www.bbc.com/news/articles/czx7kez4vx2o.

30 Randy Arrington, "Virginia's $23 Billion National Park Economy Faces Staffing Crisis," *Page Valley News*, August 23, 2023, https://pagevalleynews.com/virginias-23-billion-national-park-economy-faces-staffing-crisis/.

31 Minal Bopaiah, "Diversity, Equity and Inclusion Have Failed. Belonging, Dignity and Justice Are the Future," *World Economic Forum*, February 24, 2021, https://www.weforum.org/stories/2021/02/diversity-equity-inclusion-have-failed-belonging-dignity-justice/.

32. Jean Chemnick, "Coal Plants Smother Communities of Color," *Scientific American*, March 31, 2021, https://www.scientificamerican.com/article/coal-plants-smother-communities-of-color/.

33. The White House, "Justice40 Initiative," *The White House Archives*, accessed April 13, 2025, https://bidenwhitehouse.archives.gov/environmentaljustice/justice40/.

34. U.S. Department of Energy, "Office of State and Community Energy Programs," *U.S. Department of Energy*, accessed April 13, 2025, https://www.energy.gov/scep/office-state-and-community-energy-programs.

35. U.S. Department of Energy, "Weatherization Assistance Program," *U.S. Department of Energy*, accessed April 13, 2025, https://www.energy.gov/scep/wap/weatherization-assistance-program.

36. Nada Hassanein, "Trump Has Canceled Environmental Justice Grants. Here's What Communities Are Losing," *Stateline*, April 14, 2025, https://stateline.org/2025/04/14/trump-has-canceled-environmental-justice-grants-heres-what-communities-are-losing/.

37. Isa Gonzalez-Montilla, "Executive Order Removing Environmental Justice Tool Creates Challenges for Homebuyers," *Click2Houston*, March 19, 2025. https://www.click2houston.com/news/local/2025/03/20/trump-executive-order-removing-environmental-justice-tool-creates-challenges-for-homebuyers/.

38. U.S. Environmental Protection Agency, "Cumulative Impacts Research," *EPA*, accessed April 13, 2025, https://www.epa.gov/healthresearch/cumulative-impacts-research.

39. Minnesota Pollution Control Agency, "Cumulative Impacts Analysis," *Minnesota Pollution Control Agency*, accessed April 13, 2025, https://www.pca.state.mn.us/trending-topics/cumulative-impacts-analysis.

Conclusion

1. James Bickerton, "Gen Z Republican Support Surges, Poll Shows," *Newsweek*, April 12, 2025, https://www.newsweek.com/republican-support-poll-young-gen-z-2060258.

2. Clifton B. Parker, "Political Party Identities Stronger Than Race or Religion," *Stanford News*, August 21, 2017, https://news.stanford.edu/stories/2017/08/political-party-identities-stronger-race-religion/.

3   Harvard Kennedy School Institute of Politics, "50th Edition—Spring 2025," *Harvard IOP Youth Poll*, April 2025, https://iop.harvard.edu/youth-poll/50th-edition-spring-2025.

4   Ezra Klein, "David Shor Explains Why Trump's Electoral Path Is More Viable Than Democrats Want to Admit," *The Ezra Klein Show*, *The New York Times*, March 18, 2025, https://www.nytimes.com/2025/03/18/opinion/ezra-klein-podcast-david-shor.html.

5   Edoardo Campanella and Robert Z. Lawrence, "The Populist Revolt Against Climate Policy," *Foreign Affairs*, March/April 2024, https://www.foreignaffairs.com/united-states/populist-revolt-against-climate-policy.

6   Bradley J. Birzer, "Craig Shirley Emerges at Very Top of Reagan Biographers," *The American Conservative*, December 15, 2020, https://www.theamericanconservative.com/craig-shirley-emerges-at-very-top-of-reagan-biographers/.

7   Turning Point USA, "Our Mission," *Turning Point USA*, accessed April 13, 2025, https://www.tpusa.com/ourmission.

8   Craig Gilbert, "Biden Aims to Refocus Anger on GOP," *Milwaukee Journal Sentinel*, October 15, 2010, https://archive.jsonline.com/news/milwaukee/105078004.html.

9   "Quote by Alan Watts: 'Through Our Eyes, the Universe is Perceiving Itself . . .,'" *Goodreads*, qccessed July 11, 2025, https://www.goodreads.com/quotes/226051-through-our-eyes-the-universe-is-perceiving-itself-through-our.

10 "Quote by Carl Sagan: 'The Cosmos is Within Us. We are Made of Star-stuff . . .,'" *Goodreads*, accessed July 11, 2025, https://www.goodreads.com/quotes/484665-the-cosmos-is-within-us-we-are-made-of-star-stuff.

INDEX

adaptation; *see also* disasters—
    preparedness and resilience
    definition   69–70
    examples   69–73
    IPCC report on cities and settlements/human vulnerability   72
Advanced Research Projects Agency-Energy (ARPA-E)   164
AI and data centers
    power demand   15–16, 22, 25
    grid impacts   22

Biden, President Joe
    2020 voter turnout   16
    climate legacy   24
    environmental justice legacy   183–9
Bipartisan Infrastructure Law (BIL)   24, 66, 75, 100, 167, 184, 186
Burton, Kelly Ward   132
    fundamental human truths   132
    RAIN mindfulness meditation technique   135
The Business Case for Climate Policymaking   162–7

carbon
    bioenergy with carbon capture and storage (BECCS)   102
    Blue nature-based solutions   103–4
    credits   2
    Dioxide Removal (CDR)   3, 58
    ecological footprint   48
    footprint BP   48–9, 137
    Negative Emissions Technologies (NETs)   30, 58
    sink   69, 97–103
    source   97
Carson, Rachel   43
Castro, Chris   184
Chakraborty, Sweta
    We don't have time organization   136
CHIPS and Science Act   66, 75
Citizens Climate Lobby (CCL)   153
Clean Air Act (CAA)   43
clean/renewable energy
    Inflation Reduction Act (IRA)   5–6, 22–4, 66, 75, 184–6
    International Renewable Energy Agency (IRENA)   30
    jobs   6–7, 21–2
    offshore wind industry   21–2
Clean Industrial Revolution   52, 165–7
Clean Water Act (CWA)   43
Climate Activism 2.0   20, 43, 45, 194
climate anxiety
    2021 survey of 10,000 young adults   18
    American Psychiatric Association polls   5
    combating   41, 135
    Harvard Youth Poll   193
    more than a buzzword   40

Climate Change Means
  campaign 91–5
climate finance
  Green Climate Fund (GCF) 70
  Loss and Damage fund 76
Cook Political Report
  2026 Race Ratings 116

disasters—preparedness; *see also*
  adaptation and resilience
  "Act of God" events 85–6
  Canadian wildfires 78
  definition 69–70
  Government Accountability
    Office (GAO) report 83
  Housing and Urban Development
    (HUD) disaster and resilience
    planning role 84, 189
  Hurricane Beryl 78
  Hurricane Helene 80–1
  Hurricane Katrina 21–2, 80–1, 94, 108
  Lahaina 82–3
  Los Angeles fires 15, 81
  Phoenix heat study 79
  urban conflagration 81–2

emissions
  cement and steel 165–6
  Covid impact 53
  from energy generation 16, 26–8 (*see also* fossil fuels)
  hard to abate industrial
    sectors 165–7
  impact of President Trump 18
  impact on air pollution and public
    health 25–7, 31
  from US exports 28–9
  US historical responsibility 5
  US reduction plans/global goals
    (*see also* Paris Agreement and
    Mitigation)

energy
  addition 16–17
  demand growth US/global 15–16, 19–20
  emergency 20–2
  Energy Information Agency
    (EIA) 15–16
  exports 23, 25–7, 29
  grid—reliability 22
  imports 29, 65
  independence 20–1
  International Energy Agency
    (IEA) 6, 15
  security 6, 27–30
  transition 16–18, 31, 77, 184, 194
  UN Sustainable Development
    Goals (SDGs) 17–18
Environmental Justice
  Climate and Economic Justice
    Screening Tool 187
  Community Action Agencies
    (CAAs) 185
  community resilience hubs 190
  cumulative impacts 187–8
  Economic Opportunity Act 185
  energy burden 61
  Energy Conservation Policy
    Act 185
  Environmental Justice Screen and
    Mapping Tool 187
  Justice40 Initiative 184, 186
  Low Income Home Energy
    Assistance Program
    (LIHEAP) 8, 189
  Public Environmental Data
    Partners 187
  State and Community Energy
    Programs (SCEPs) 184, 188–9
  urban extreme heat
    exposure 61, 73
  Weatherization Assistance
    Program (WAP) 184, 186

Weatherization Readiness Fund
(WRF)   189
Environmental Protection Agency
(EPA)   26, 43, 61, 160, 187
Environmental Voter Project   131

fossil fuels
American Petroleum Institute
(API)   16
divestment movement   114
Organization of the Petroleum
Exporting Countries
(OPEC)   27
petroleum definition   27
projections through
midcentury   6–7, 15–18, 30
short note on coal   25–7
subsidies   29–31, 65, 120, 161, 168

Gates, Bill
Green Premiums   165–7
Georgetown University
Business for Impact, Georgetown
McDonough School of
Business   89
Crutchfield, Leslie   89, 96
Georgetown Climate Center   9
Institute of Politics and Public
Service democracy poll   5
Gore, Al
Climate Reality Project   153
Green New Deal   65

Hayoe, Katherine   123–5
House Select Committee on the
Climate Crisis
Solving the Climate Crisis: The
Congressional Action Plan for
a Clean Energy Economy and
a Healthy, Resilient, and Just
America   66, 75
Humboldt, Alexander von   44

Intergovernmental Panel on Climate
Change (IPCC)   72–3, 77,
102, 142
issue identification
definition-how to increase   37–9,
51, 83, 95–7
IMF global study of 30,000
respondents   38–9
Pew Research Center studies on
Americans' views on climate
change   34–6
policy windows   161
role in overcoming
polarization   39
role in overcoming voter
disengagement   132, 137

Johnson, Ayana   5

Kirk, Charlie—Turning Point
USA   118–22
Klein, Ezra   130, 159

Levelized Cost of Energy
(LCOE)   14
loss and damage
definition   75–6
examples   77–82
low-propensity voters   130–1
Luntz, Frank
ask-a-question rule of effective
language   91, 96

Mind Body Ecology Institute
(MBEI)   135
Mitigation
American Council for an Energy-
Efficient Economy (ACEEE)
US cities report   141
Brookings Institution 100 largest
cities emissions reduction
targets report   141

Definition 69
Examples 69–71
Long-Term Strategy of the United States: Pathways to Net-Zero Greenhouse Gas Emissions by 2050 (LTS) 102–3
Mid-Century Strategy for deep decarbonization (MCS) 98–102

Net Zero 2, 30–1, 102–4
The New Climate Denialism 12–15, 20, 51, 201
Newton's Third Law of Politics 118–22
Nuckels, Ben 110–14, 117

Obama, President Barack
 all-of-the-above energy policy 23–4
 marriage equality 197
 US decarbonization plans 98–9
One Trillion Trees 97–105
Operation Rescue anti-abortion campaign 87–8
Oxfam International carbon footprint example 49–50

Parental Activism
 Moms for Liberty (M4L) 144–5, 149
Paris Agreement
 global goals and timeline 24, 29, 56–60, 70
 Kerry, John 162–4
 Ratchet Mechanism 57
 US goal—Nationally Determined Contribution (NDC) 7–8
Posner, Alex
 EcoRight conservative movement 114

Students for Carbon Dividends 115
Potential Energy Coalition
 "future gens" messaging 125–6
Project 2025 164
Project Drawdown 65
public lands conservation
 Antiquities Act 174–6
 impact of President Theodore Roosevelt 174
 National Parks Conservation Association (NPCA) 181
 Outdoor Industry Association (OIA) 179
 Outdoor Recreation Economy and the impact of protected lands to job creation in surrounding communities 178–81
 Western Governors' Association report 179
 Wilderness Act 177

Rait, Ken 176–8
Reagan, President Ronald 95, 174
 Shirley, Craig 195–9
Recency Bias 18
resilience; *see also* adaptation and disasters—preparedness
 Chief Resilience Officer 85
 Dual-benefit 74–5
 National Flood Insurance Program (NFIP) 85
 National Institute of Building Sciences report 71
 US Chamber of Commerce report 71
Ritchie, Hannah 11–12, 109

Sagan, Carl 202
Schwartz, Tony
 Responsive Cord theory 91, 96

Shane, Courtney Durham 76–7
Strait, Elan
 Michigan clean energy standard 150–2
 we are still in coalition 8–10, 142–3
subnational actors
 definition 10
 commitment to Paris Agreement goals 8–11, 142

Thunberg, Greta 49
Tragedy of the Commons 161–2

United Nations Framework Convention on Climate Change
 COP23 9–10
 goal 59–60
 Kyoto Protocol 59

US Forest Service "Roadless Rule" 171, 177
 Tongass National Forest, Alaska 170, 180
USDA Building Blocks for Climate Smart Agriculture and Forestry 102
 precision agriculture and agroforestry 101

Watts, Alan 202
Wolfson, Evan
 Freedom to Marry campaign 88–90, 197

Yale Program on Climate Change Communications
 Global Warming's Six Americas study 123–5

ABOUT THE AUTHOR

Will Hackman served as a political fundraiser and campaign manager on four federal races for the US House and Senate as well as a gubernatorial campaign. In 2013, he joined the public sector nonprofit community as a marine fisheries conservation advocate for a global nonpartisan organization dedicated to addressing the challenges of a changing world. Will first developed a love for the ocean as a commercial Alaskan salmon fisherman during the summers while in college. He later completed a season commercially fishing for Alaskan Bering Sea crab—one of the most dangerous jobs in the world. Since 2013, Will has served as a senior strategist in conservation advocacy efforts and has helped to advance public policies related to ocean and land conservation as well as clean energy and the environment.

Among his many efforts, Will spent years defending Alaska's Tongass National Forest from industrial logging—the United States' largest national forest and one of the world's largest temperate rainforests, worked with local and indigenous communities across the western United States on public lands and rivers conservation efforts, helped strengthen fuel-efficiency regulations for cars and trucks, helped pass major bipartisan legislation to combat illegal fishing, and has engaged in international marine fisheries conservation efforts around the world.

Will regularly attends UN and other climate conferences and is a contributing author on energy, environmental, and climate change topics for print, podcasts, and online media. Will has been published in *The Washington Post*, *The Hill*, *Anchorage Daily News*, *Georgetown Journal of International Affairs*, *Georgetown Public Policy Review*, and other outlets. He was a contributing author among other experts in global climate communications and media to a 2024 whitepaper on creating a "New Era in Climate Communications." His 2022 TEDx "The Future of Climate Change is Personal" challenges us to reframe our climate conversations to overcome polarization and partisanship. Will lives in the beautiful Shenandoah Valley in Front Royal, Virginia, with his wife Paula, tucked into the Blue Ridge Mountains and the north entrance to Shenandoah National Park.

Will graduated from Bradley University in Peoria, Illinois, in 2007 with a bachelor's degree in international studies and received his master's in public policy from Georgetown University's McCourt School in 2018.